I dedicate this book to the memory of my father . . . as a gift of my love.

Table of Contents

Chapter 1

❦

Farmers Daughter

Carolyn was a happy baby.

She lived on a farm in the green hills of Vermont with her Mommy and Daddy and her older brother, Douglas. She was happy because she received plenty of love and attention. Mommy understood her needs even though Carolyn couldn't talk yet except to say Mama or Dada.

Mommy always dressed her in frilly dresses. Carolyn didn't have much hair, but what she did have Mommy fastened a pretty ribbon on, tied in a bow.

It was a big farmhouse, but the family only lived in part of it. During the long winter months the closed off rooms were very cold, but now in May they were only cool.

The living room and Mommy and Daddy's bedroom had varnished hardwood floors that shone because Mommy kept them polished, just like the doors and baseboards. The back bedroom where Dougie slept had wide floor boards covered with linoleum.

A tall, brown kerosene stove heated the living room, the bathroom and the two bedrooms. The distinctive black stove pipe curved loftily upward until it disappeared through a round hole in the ceiling.

Carolyn sat on the floor while Mommy shut the kerosene stove off. The spring nights were cool, so in the evening and all night the stove was on low. When the strong morning sunlight streamed through the wide living room windows Mommy could shut the heater off. However, on rainy days it was a different matter. The dampness penetrated every nook and cranny of the drafty old farmhouse.

Every morning, Mommy cleaned the black soot that collected on the little window in the front of the stove. First, she turned the outside knob to swing it open. With a piece of tissue paper she would wipe it clean. She threw the soiled paper into the fire. The eager flames licked it up quickly before Mommy could shut the window. Then she closed the outer door before going around behind the stove to turn the off switch.

Mommy frequently warned Carolyn about the dangers of the hot stove. She told her never to touch it because it would burn her hand. Sometimes Mommy would pick Carolyn up to give her a peek through the little round window. Carolyn would watch in fascination as the orange and red flames danced. She could feel the heat from them on her face.

Next it was time for Carolyn's breakfast.

Mommy scooped her darling little girl into her arms. She carried her down the hall into the kitchen. The hall and kitchen were part of the original house built in the late 1700's. The floors were wood, worn to a gray from all the times they had been washed.

The kitchen and pantry, where the sink and cupboards were, had wide floor boards covered with linoleum. That area was heated by a huge black and white cook stove that used wood.

Mommy placed Carolyn in her high chair. Then she turned to cut thick slices off the loaf of homemade bread. She placed them on the top of the cook stove, which was called the griddle, to toast them.

Carolyn liked them that way. With a metal spatula Mommy pressed the pieces of bread flat, letting them brown lightly before flipping them over to toast on the other side. The fragrance of sweet dough filled the whole kitchen. Mommy slid them neatly onto a plate. She placed it on the kitchen table to butter them.

Carolyn's mouth watered while she watched. She reached one chubby hand out to grab a piece of toast but they were too far away, even though Mommy was standing right next to the high chair.

Mommy spread homemade strawberry jam on top of the butter and placed one half slice on the high chair tray. Enthusiastically, Carolyn bit into it. The taste was delightfully sweet. The jam was sticky. The fresh butter made her fingers and face greasy. Happily, she took another bite.

When Daddy came in from the barn he said, "It's going to be a nice day if it don't rain." It was the first thing he said every morning, rain or shine. The first time he said it he was being quite sincere, but Dougie thought it was funny. He laughed until his sides ached. After that, Daddy made his prediction of the day every morning when he entered the house.

He never came in the house in his smelly barn overalls or boots. He took them off outside the door and left them in the woodshed. He hung his coat on a hook behind the hall door. He went directly from there to the pantry sink where he washed his hands, arms, neck, face and bald head before he sat down to eat breakfast.

"Do you have to go downstreet today?" Daddy asked Mommy.

Downstreet was three miles away to the village of Richmond. Even though it was a small town it had an IGA store.

"Yes, I need to buy some meat," Mommy replied.

So after the breakfast dishes were done Daddy walked down the road to the old horse barn. The barn no longer housed horses. It stored Daddy's tractor and other farm equipment.

Daddy had converted the front part of the barn to a garage. He backed the 1948 Ford Coupe out of the converted horse barn and drove it the few feet down to the driveway where Mommy and Carolyn were waiting.

The car was five years old, but it was new to them since they had only recently bought it. It had low mileage, a nice interior and no rust: the three things that Daddy always looked for when he needed a car.

Mommy didn't know how to drive, so whenever she needed to go to town Daddy brought her. Doug sat in the backseat, but Carolyn sat on Mommy's lap in the front seat where she could see the pretty green hills and valleys. She always enjoyed the ride to town.

Children are a gift from God; they are his reward. Psalm 127:3

Chapter 2

❦

The Nail

Carolyn crawled through the living room.

She heard her mother and father talking in the kitchen and she wanted to be with them even though what they were talking about didn't interest her. It was their company that she longed for.

But the day before as she crawled down the hall that led to the kitchen, her bare knee encountered the head of a nail. She stopped to look at it.

It wasn't a large nail. Only the tip of the head was raised up from the floor board it was nailed to. The hall, like the kitchen, wasn't varnished. The wood, more than a century old, was weathered and worn.

Her knee hadn't suffered any damage. But now that she knew about the nail she felt for it first with her hand. When she found it she crawled around it. Smugly, she continued toward her destination.

Every day after dinner Mommy sat in one of the four wooden chairs that matched the kitchen table. Daddy sat in the chrome rocking chair by the window and smoked one of the cigarettes Mommy rolled for him. They talked about everyday matters. Soon, Daddy would leave the warm kitchen to go back outside to work. Mommy would bake or clean until it was time to make supper.

It was cozy in the kitchen. The wood stove was hot, the tea kettle on it was steaming. The kitchen smelled of food, coffee and smoke.

Carolyn crawled up to Mommy and sat on the floor at her feet. She listened to them talk. She felt safe with Mommy and Daddy.

When Daddy left Mommy got Carolyn ready for her nap. First she changed her diapers. Mommy always put her finger inside Carolyn's diaper when she pinned it so that she could protect Carolyn from a pin prick. Next came the rubber pants. Mommy smoothed Carolyn's dress down over them. Then she picked her up.

Carolyn wrapped her arms around her Mommy's neck.

"Give Mommy a kiss night night, honey."

Carolyn gave Mommy a wet kiss before she was laid down on the mattress in the yellow crib. Mommy covered her with a soft, warm blanket. Carolyn put her left thumb in her mouth and was instantly asleep.

When Carolyn woke up from her nap Dougie was in the barn helping Daddy with the chores. Supper was sizzling on the stove. A yellow cake with chocolate frosting was sitting on the counter in the pantry.

While Mommy waited for the men to come in from the barn she rocked and sang to Carolyn in the chrome chair in the kitchen. Carolyn liked to be rocked. She patted Mommy's face as she sang to her.

Several days went by and Carolyn continued to outsmart the nail. Then one day as she crawled down the hall her hand missed the familiar raised head. No matter. She was too smart to let the nail hurt her knee a second time.

She crawled on. Suddenly the nail reared its ugly head against Carolyn's unsuspecting knee. At the sharp pierce of pain she began to cry.

To Mommy's experienced ears she knew right away that Carolyn was hurt. When she reached her she saw that her knee was bleeding.

"Ray, come here. Carolyn's been cut, but I don't see anything in the hall that could have done it."

With Dougie helping, Daddy searched the hall. Mommy brought Carolyn into the pantry where she sat her on the counter next to the sink so she could wash the blood off her knee and bandage it.

"A nail has worked loose. I'll have to go out to my workshop to get a hammer. I'll be right back," Daddy said.

A minute later Daddy was pounding the nail back in place. Even with a bandage on her knee Carolyn was afraid to leave the safety of Mommy's arms. She clung to her desperately, refusing to crawl.

"Let's go see what Daddy is doing."

"Here's where that nail was. I pounded it in so it can never hurt my baby again."

Daddy smiled at Carolyn as she looked at him through tragic blue eyes, a tear drop still on her lashes.

"See, honey, it's alright. Daddy won't let it ever hurt you again." He touched her soft cheek with his thumb to wipe the tears away.

Like as a father pitieth his children, so the Lord pitieth them that reverence him. Psalm 103:13

Chapter 3

Betty

"I've decided to sell my farm, Ray."

A neighbor had come to see Daddy. His name was Barney O'Toole. He was a friend.

"My boys don't have any interest in running it," Daddy's friend said sadly. "They've all got good jobs in the city. I'm getting too old to run it by myself. It was different when the Missus was alive. There's no point in staying on there now that she's gone." He paused for a minute before he continued. "I'll come right to the point of my visit. I know how you've often admired my dog, Betty. You've seen her work. I trained her myself to bring the cows home to the barn at milking time. She wouldn't be happy laying around a small house in town with nothing to do. I hate like heck to give her up, but there it is. I've thought about it ever since I made the decision to sell and there's nobody else I'd give her to 'cept you. She's yours if you want her."

Daddy accepted the offer gladly. He had seen her work on the other man's farm. At milking time she would go into the meadow, round up the cows and head them for home. A good cow dog could save the farmer time and energy.

The next day Mr. O'Toole brought her over.

"She's part bird dog and part Shepherd. She loves to chase birds or anything else. She'll make a good watch dog for you when she gets use to the place. Until then you should probably tie her up at night. Otherwise she might take it in her head to come back to my farm. She's never known no other home."

Betty's hair was long and black except under her chin where it was tan color. Her feet and snout were white as well as the tip of her tail.

That night Daddy tied twine around Betty's collar. He tied the other end to a stake in the ground. She howled at the moon for a bit. Then all was quiet. But the next morning Daddy discovered that Betty had chewed through the twine.

After the barn chores were done and breakfast eaten Daddy left for Mr. O'Toole's house.

The place had the feel of death about it. The death of a dream, the death of a farm.

"Thought you'd be coming by for her, Ray, as soon as I'd seen she'd come back." He shoved his big, rough hands into his pockets. He looked over at his barn.

"Sold my herd yesterday. They're headed for the slaughter house, I guess. My tools and equipment go on the auction block this weekend." There was deep, resolute sadness in his voice.

"Why did you have to sell everything? Didn't the people you sold the farm to need any of the animals and equipment, or are they bringing their own?"

"Sold it to a retired doctor from New York. He and

his wife want this place only as a summer house. They stink of money. Probably won't recognize it once they're done with it."

He looked over the barn and fields, then the farm-house. "It was a good farm once. We made a fair living off of it. Raised five healthy children. That's all behind me now." His head dropped. He kicked at a stone in the road. It went flying.

Daddy waited until Mr. O'Toole could compose himself. He knew what despair his friend was feeling.

"You've been a good neighbor, Ray, and a good friend." The two men shook hands solemnly. Then Mr. O'Toole said, "Sure hope Betty works out for you. I don't think the new owner will like her showing up on his doorstep."

Mr. O'Toole gave Betty a final scratch on the head. "Good bye, old girl."

That night Daddy tied Betty with a heavy rope. "She isn't going to be able to chew her way through it this time."

The next morning all that was left at the end of the rope was the collar.

Before Daddy had time to finish the chores Mr. O'Toole brought her back. "When I come out of my house this morning she was asleep on the front step. I don't know what you're going to do with her, Ray. I'm afraid if you tried to keep her inside either the house or the barn she'd jump straight through a window."

"I'll keep tying her up at night. If she's gone in the morning I'll go over to your place and bring her back home. Maybe once you leave and she knows you aren't coming back, then she'll decide to stick around here."

"I'm sure sorry for all the trouble she's caused you so far. I'd hoped she would make you a good dog."

"Could be she's a one man dog, Barney. Only time will tell."

Every night for two weeks she escaped and every day Daddy drove the car up the road, got her and brought her back home. Then one morning the new people were there.

Daddy introduced himself. "Hello, my name is Raymond Dupont. I live down the hill on the next farm. This is my wife, Pearl, my son, Douglas and my daughter, Carolyn."

"My name is Doctor Devereaux. This is my wife, Mrs. Devereaux." He looked very out of place in his double-breasted suit.

"Are you here to ask about the hay crop? The former owner mentioned you might be interested in it." Then he told Daddy the terms. "If you agree to keep my fence lines up, including the stone fences, keep the weeds to a minimum, tend my apple orchard, then you can cut the hay and keep it in trade. Agreed?"

Daddy recovered from his surprise quickly. He hadn't expected this proposition. "I can use the hay," he said, "and I'll keep your fences up as long as I can put in a gate between my land and yours so that I can have easy access to your fields. I'll mow the front part of the apple orchard and take the hay from it, but you'll have to tend to your own trees or just leave them be."

"Alright then. By the way, do you know anything about this dog? She's become quite a nuisance. Every time my wife and I approach the house she growls at us. We're afraid she's going to bite."

While Daddy explained the situation to the elderly couple, Dougie was attracted to the new Buick they had parked in their driveway. It had a big, shiny chrome bumper. Dougie could see his reflection in it when he walked back and forth in front of it. He looked very small.

Daddy called to Doug. "Time to go home, son." Doug crawled into the back seat, Mommy and Carolyn were in the front. Since Betty refused to come when Daddy called her he had to go after her. He put the collar around her neck, took it in his hand and began to bring her over to the car. Her four legs were stiff and she kept looking back at the Devereaux's, growling at them as if to say this was her property and they were trespassers. She got into the back seat with Doug reluctantly.

Daddy turned the car around in the middle of the road. As he did the family got a glimpse of the doctor. He was wiping the chrome bumper on his car with a white handkerchief, even though Douglas hadn't touched it.

"I guess he thinks he can wipe off Doug's image," Daddy remarked with his dry Yankee humor.

When they reached home Daddy said, "Now that the Devereaux's have arrived we can't continue like this. I've been thinking. It seems to me that my grandfather told me once about a dog he had in Ireland that kept running away. He said that he buttered all four of her paws. After that she didn't run away any more. I'd like to try it on Betty. I'd have to bring her into the kitchen to do it. Is that alright with you?"

"We have nothing to lose by trying it," Mommy said.

Carolyn sat on the floor watching with great interest while Daddy buttered Betty's feet. It was a funny sight to see him lift each paw and smear it with butter. Betty didn't seem to mind. At first, she sniffed the butter, then Daddy, but after that she lay quietly on her side, her head resting on the floor.

When he finished he said, "My grandfather told

me when I was a little boy that this is a sure-fire cure for a runaway dog. If she licks the butter off all four paws then she'll never run away again."

"What if she doesn't?" Dougie asked.

"Then it didn't work and we'll have to try it again later. I don't know what else to do."

"Let's sit down at the table to give her some privacy, but where we can watch to see what she does."

A minute or two later Betty began to lick one paw on her hind leg. Then slowly she began on the other one. Finally, she licked her front paws. She even licked the butter stains on the floor.

Daddy gave her plenty of time. She licked each paw several more times. When she finished she went to the door.

Daddy was all smiles as he stood up from the table. "Well, that does it then. We won't tie her up tonight. We'll wait and see if this does the trick."

After Daddy left with Betty, Mommy got out her metal bucket and a heavy brush. She scrubbed the butter stain until her arms ached, but it didn't go away. For many months it stood as a silent reminder of the Irish grandfather and his cure for a runaway dog.

Those that thou gavest me I have kept, and none of them is lost . . . John 17:12b

Chapter 4

Grandpa

Grandpa Dupont had come for a visit.

Not that he lived so very far away, because he didn't. His home was in Winooski, a distance of not more than 30 miles. But it was summertime and hot in the city. And besides, his one true love was farming.

Years before, after he and his wife sold the boarding house they owned, he built her a small one story house to live in. It was nice, but he felt freer away from the city, here on his son's farm.

Since Grandpa was French-Canadian the children called him Pepe, which means Grandfather in French.

Pepe was very tall, much taller than Daddy. He was over 6 feet and he had huge hands. He was old, but still very strong. He had been a farmer for much of his life, and during the lean years after he lost his barn and animals in a fire, he was a house painter in Massachusetts. He had a long reach and could paint equally well with either hand. He was in great demand because he could finish a house quicker than any other painter.

Daddy's house needed to be painted. He could afford the white paint for it, but not someone to do the work. Since he was busy day and night with the crops on his farm and the doctor's farm land, too, he didn't have time to paint it himself. Pepe decided to help him get the job done.

High on the ladder he climbed with a bucket of paint and his brush. He began at the peak of the house, two stories high. Since it was a small area he quickly finished it. As he moved down the ladder the house became wider. He dipped the brush in the paint, then he painted the right side, down and then back. He dipped the brush in the paint again. Switching hands he repeated what he had done on the other side. He finished the area before moving down to the next rung on the ladder. In no time at all he had the front section completed.

When Pepe was a younger man he could paint all day. Now, at almost seventy, his legs grew tired standing on the rungs of the ladder. Daddy and Mommy were afraid for him, so he promised that he wouldn't overdo it. He would paint only in the morning.

He covered the paint bucket, pounding the lid into place with a hammer. Then he removed the ladder from where it was leaning against the house. He put it in the workshop where the children wouldn't be likely to get hurt by it accidentally. Then he carefully cleaned his brush until he was certain that no paint remained in it. He set it on newspapers to dry.

After lunch Daddy took his tractor up to the neighbor's farm to mow their hay. Daddy had an agreement with the New York doctor that if he kept their fields mowed he could keep the hay.

Pepe sat in the kitchen rocking chair smoking his pipe contentedly. His grandchildren played at his feet. His son was running a successful farm. He liked his daughter-in-law. She was a fine woman and she made his son a good wife.

"Anything I can do for you, Pearl?" he asked Mommy.

"How would you like to take Doug strawberry picking? I'll make strawberry shortcake for supper tonight, if you pick me enough."

"That's my favorite," he said, but Mommy already knew that.

Wild strawberries grew in abundance along the hillside next to the farmhouse. Pepe had a long stride that matched his lanky frame. Dougie had to take two steps to keep up with every step Pepe took.

When the kindly old gentleman noticed he slowed down. There was no rush. They had all afternoon to pick strawberries.

Plunk, into the tin pail they hit until the bottom was no longer visible. Then the ripe juicy red berries began to grow inside until the two pails were filled to the brim and yet there were many more strawberries left to be picked another day.

Dougie was filled to the brim, too. The sweet strawberries were too much of a temptation for the little boy. For every two he picked, one had found its way into his mouth. Strawberries were his favorite, too.

Together, man and boy walked back to the house. The afternoon sun was warm on their backs. The sweet smell of strawberries filled the air. A crow broke the silence with its piercing caw. A bee buzzed past Pepe's ear on its way home. The brook sang of its own mysteries as it wound its way through the meadow.

Pepe heard the John Deere tractor coming down the hill. He and Dougie walked out from the meadow, onto the dirt road. They waited by the side until Daddy stopped the tractor next to them.

Dougie climbed up the back of the tractor to reach the seat next to Daddy. Pepe stepped onto the back of the tractor hitch. One hand held onto the back of Daddy's seat, the other held the two pails of strawberries.

When the men came into the house Mommy's biscuits were already in the oven. For dessert the bottom half of the biscuit would get filled with the cleaned, sugared berries. Then the top half would be placed on with lots more berries added. For the finishing touch the whole thing would be smothered by a pile of fresh whipped cream.

After supper Pepe pushed his chair back and smiled. "That was the best strawberry shortcake I ever had," he said. "But don't tell Meme I said that."

While Pepe painted the house Dougie was never too far away. Daddy was busy in the fields, Mommy was making strawberry jam from the berries Pepe and Doug picked for her every afternoon.

Carolyn spent most of her time in a walker, learning how to walk. When her legs got too tired to continue she had a convenient seat in the walker in which to sit down on. Also, it kept her occupied and out of harm's way.

The one obstacle that Carolyn constantly came up against was the little hill that separated the kitchen from the living room. It was just steep enough to cause Carolyn to have to push against the heavy walker in order to get to the top. It was hard for her to do, even though it wasn't more than a step for an adult. She worked at it constantly because it was so much fun to ride back down the hill. It tickled her tummy.

The week was over. The whole house was freshly painted. Pepe was sitting in the kitchen rocking chair smoking his pipe. Tomorrow he would go back home. Pepe watched Carolyn struggle up the small incline. Feeling sorry for her he went over to the walker and placed his foot against the bottom where the wheels were. He gave her a small shove and suddenly she was at the top of the hill. Delighted she turned the walker around for the ride back down.

When she came to the hill again she looked back over her shoulder at her grandfather. "Eah, eah," she said. Laughing, he got up to push her again. Every time after that she waited for him to come help her. But he didn't mind. She was, after all, his baby granddaughter.

The next day when Pepe brought his suitcase to the car Dougie started to cry. Pepe picked him up in his arms to give him a hug.

"I'll be back," he told the little boy.

Next, Pepe shook hands with Daddy. Daddy put his free hand on his father's shoulder. "Thank you, Pa," he said.

Mommy gave Pepe a quart of strawberries to bring home with him and some fresh strawberry jam.

"They won't taste as good in the city as they did here," he told her. He touched Carolyn's cheek with his forefinger. Bashfully, she buried her face in Mommy's shoulder.

Pepe took one last look around before getting into the car. The white house sparkled in the sunlight. He had done that for his son. He had given him so little and in return he had received so much.

He waved as he pulled out of the driveway and headed the car for home.

> *He is kind and merciful—and all goes well for the generous man who conducts his business fairly. He gives generously to those in need. His deeds will never be forgotten.* Psalms 112:5 and 9.

Chapter 5

Dougie

When Carolyn was a year old she started to walk.

At first she pulled herself up holding onto the couch, a table or a chair. Then she would steady herself, get her balance, take a couple of steps with her arms outstretched before plopping down on her behind. It didn't hurt because God specially padded it for just such a purpose. Also, her diaper helped cushion the fall.

Stubbornly, Carolyn would crawl over to the couch again, pull herself up, turn around resting her back against the support of the couch until she was certain of her balance and then she would take a step. Each time she had a little more confidence, a little more self-control.

Every day Mommy and Douglas helped Carolyn practice her walking. Douglas, who was already five years old, held onto Carolyn's hands. Mommy was across the room with her arms outstretched.

"Come to me, Carolyn," Mommy said with a smile. Her soft brown eyes twinkled lovingly. "You can do it."

Carolyn let go of Dougie's fingers. Hesitantly at first she took some steps toward Mommy. Part way there she stopped to catch her balance again. Mommy urged her on. Carolyn laughed. It was a fun game.

Sometimes Carolyn fell before reaching Mommy. Then Dougie picked her up and they tried it again. Carolyn loved it when Mommy's solid arms finally encircled her. Then Mommy turned Carolyn around to face Dougie. He held his arms out to her. She caught her balance, let go of Mommy and headed toward Doug. Part way there she changed her mind, turned around and went back to Mommy.

Each day Carolyn's legs got stronger. Then one day it happened. Daddy was sitting in his rocking chair watching the news on the black and white Motorola television set. Carolyn sat next to Mommy on the couch. She decided that she wanted to be rocked on Daddy's lap. She rolled her body to the edge of the couch letting her feet touch the floor before she let go with her hands. She walked across the room to Daddy. She hardly realized what she had accomplished until everyone began to cheer. Daddy picked her up on his lap and kissed her soft, round cheek. Carolyn had walked the whole length of the room.

After that Carolyn only crawled if she wanted to get someplace quickly, like if she spotted a toy. Otherwise she walked.

Sunday morning she held Mommy's hand and walked into church. She and Mommy always sat in the cry room with the other babies. The whole front of the room was made out of glass so they could see the priest on the altar. Sometimes the sound was adjusted so they could hear the Mass and other times it wasn't. It was funny watching the priest, but not being able to hear him. Carolyn liked that best, but Mommy didn't. She complained afterwards that it didn't feel like she had even gone to church.

Carolyn never cried in the cry room, but other babies did. Lots of times it was noisy. Mommy sat in the front row with Carolyn on her lap. Daddy and Douglas always met them at the door to the cry room after church was over.

"Next Sunday I'm going to sit with you," Mommy said. "I'm tired of not being able to hear the priest say the Mass. If the speaker is turned on the babies are too noisy. Carolyn is good. She can sit on my lap."

Daddy agreed. He wanted his wife to sit with him again.

Sunday dinners were special. Mommy stuffed a chicken. While the family was at church the bird would cook in the oven of the black and white wood stove.

When the family came home the good smell of baked chicken greeted them at the door.

Carolyn was a good eater. She sat in the wooden

high chair between Mommy and Daddy. She had a plastic bowl that Daddy filled with chicken, dressing, mashed potatoes, squash, and cranberry sauce. She ate with a spoon and her fingers until she had enough. Mommy washed her face and hands before releasing her from the high chair.

She and Dougie went into the living room. She was walking better every day. They played quietly for a while, but Carolyn wasn't content to sit on the floor. She wanted to try out her new found freedom. She pushed the toys aside and stood up. Dougie did too. "I'm going to get you," he told her, like he had seen Mommy do.

He started chasing her around the room. She squealed with delight. Around and around they went, passing chairs, the couch, end tables, the TV. Carolyn was running as fast as her chubby legs could go. Looking back she saw that Dougie was right behind her. He was running slowly, his hands were outstretched as though to catch her. He was smiling.

Then Mommy was in the doorway, disapproving. "Douglas," she said, "don't chase her like that. She only just learned to walk this week. Her legs might get tired and she could fall against the furniture and get hurt."

Dougie hung his head. Mommy went back into the kitchen. Carolyn ran, but Dougie didn't chase her so she went up to him. She placed her two hands against his chest and pushed. Her blue eyes were dancing. She ran a little bit away from him, paused to look back with an impish grin. That's when he started to chase her again.

They were having a lot of fun. Carolyn knew that she wasn't going to fall like Mommy feared. Her balance was better than Mommy knew. It was a fun game. She wouldn't get hurt.

Squealing and laughing they ran until Daddy came in. "I thought your mother told you not to chase her any more."

"But she wants me to, Daddy."

"Your mother is afraid she'll fall, son. She can't learn to run until she has learned to walk better."

Hope surged through Doug. "But I'm being careful. I'm teaching her how to run."

"No. I want you to stop it now."

Dougie agreed reluctantly. He leaned against the couch with a sad look on his face. Carolyn went up to him and pushed him like before, but this time he didn't chase her. Again she pushed him and again. Sadly he told her he couldn't chase her any more.

She was sorry that the fun game had ended. She knew that Dougie was sorry too. She was sure she wouldn't get hurt. She knew she could run. She wasn't the least bit tired. But she couldn't tell them because she hadn't learned how to talk yet. Dougie had tried to tell them, but they wouldn't listen. Sadly, Carolyn walked away to explore some other part of her new world.

> *For the moment all discipline seems painful rather than pleasant. Later it yields the peaceful fruit of righteousness to those who have been trained by it.* Hebrews 12:11

Chapter 6

Cousin Duane

The months passed. It was summer again.

Another Sunday morning found Mommy getting Carolyn ready for church. Carolyn was pleased that she got to wear her favorite dress.

It was yellow with little blue flowers. It had puffy short sleeves. What made it her favorite, though, was that it had three big pockets along the front. Carolyn loved keeping things in them such as stones from the driveway or flowers from the garden. At the end of the day the flowers were wilted and Mommy made her throw the stones back, but meanwhile she was free to take them out to admire whenever she wanted.

After church was over Daddy drove the family home. Carolyn and Dougie sat in the roomy back seat.

Dougie was a sturdy boy, nothing sissified about him, she often heard her mother say. He was thin and tall. His hair was black, like Carolyn's, only curly. He had brown eyes edged by generous lashes. He looked like Mommy's side of the family.

Daddy pulled the car into the converted garage. The family got out and walked down the road toward the big white farmhouse.

They were going to have company today. Anxious to check on the dinner that was cooking in the oven Mommy hurried up the steps into the wood shed, past the eight cords of wood that had been delivered yesterday. Tomorrow Daddy would start cutting the bigger chunks down to more manageable sizes on the circular saw. The house was never locked. Mommy opened the kitchen door. Inside, the heavenly aroma of stuffed chicken made Carolyn's tummy rumble.

Mommy first checked on her meal before she went and changed into a house dress. Carolyn went skipping back outside to wait for the strange company to arrive.

They weren't really strange to anyone but her. Mommy had told her that it was her sister, her sister's husband and their little boy who was only one year older than Carolyn. Mommy had assured her that she had met them before, but Carolyn couldn't remember.

Suddenly a shiny long car drove into the driveway. A man and a woman got out. They were the same size. The woman looked a little bit like Mommy, but Carolyn thought that Mommy was much prettier.

The little boy had shorts on. Carolyn had never seen such a sight before since Douglas always wore long pants.

"How are you today, Carolyn," Uncle Homer asked her with a pat, pat, pat on her head with his hand as he went by.

"Hello, Sweetie," Aunt Mabel said. She twisted Carolyn's head and planted a kiss on her cheek. Then she wiped off the lipstick with her thumb before continuing on up the steps.

"Hello, Pearl, something smells good." That was Uncle Homer as he walked into Mommy's kitchen.

Cousin Duane and Carolyn stared at each other. He smiled at her a shy smile. But she didn't smile back. She was trying to make up her mind whether she liked him or not. He wasn't very much like Dougie. He was only a little taller than her. His hair was cut short and it was brown, the same color as his eyes.

He seemed like a nice boy. Carolyn decided that she liked him. He had a red rubber ball. They sat down on the lawn across from each other with their legs open and began to roll the ball back and forth until dinnertime.

Dinner was always a joyous occasion. First, they had chicken and stuffing. Not bread stuffing either. It was hamburg stuffing with only a little toasted bread added along with Mommy's secret ingredients. They had potatoes and gravy, homemade biscuits, cranberry sauce, celery, plenty of fresh milk—Carolyn preferred hers with chocolate mixed in—and squash.

After dinner there was an array of homemade pies. Carolyn choose her favorite, blueberry. She cut into the flaky crust and down into the berries. The first forkful was delicious. Even though Carolyn was already full, she finished most of the pie. The end of the crust she left on the plate, but as she got down from the table she saw that Daddy had reached over and taken it. He finished it. She felt better about it, since she knew Mommy didn't like for her to waste good food.

The women cleared the table. Duane and Carolyn went into the living room to play. She showed him her dolls, but he wasn't much impressed. It wasn't until Dougie showed up with an armful of toy farm equipment, tractors, barns, fences, cows, horses, and other assorted animals, that all three children found a game they could enjoy playing together.

The day wore on and finally it was time for the company to leave. Carolyn wasn't sorry to see them go. She was tired. They all went outside. Duane found his ball in the front yard partially hidden by the green grass. Carolyn sat down on the middle step, her elbows on her knees, her chin resting in her hands. It was then that Aunt Mabel remembered the camera in her car.

"Homer, go get the camera. I want to take a picture."

Dutifully he brought it back. She stood on the sidelines. "You know I take dreadful pictures. You take it. I want one of Duane kissing Carolyn."

Well, that made Carolyn sit up and take notice. What if she didn't want Duane to kiss her. With Aunt Mabel coaxing him, Duane stood on the bottom step and leaned over to kiss Carolyn's cheek, like he had seen his mother do earlier in the day.

Carolyn pulled herself away just in time. Duane kissed air as Uncle Homer snapped the picture.

"Dougie, Dougie," Aunt Mabel called. "Come here and sit down next to your sister."

Carolyn was fine with that until Aunt Mabel insisted that Duane sit on the other side. She scooted as close to her brother as she could. He put his arm around her neck. It felt heavy, but she was thankful that it added a welcomed distance to Cousin Duane.

Snap, a second picture was taken. This time Carolyn even smiled a little.

But, Aunt Mabel still wasn't satisfied. "Pearl, come out here and make Carolyn sit still so that Duane can kiss her."

So Mommy came out and stood on the top step of

the woodshed. Carolyn was sitting down below, still on the middle step. Mommy said to Aunt Mabel that maybe Carolyn didn't want a kiss.

Carolyn sighed with relief, but Aunt Mabel wouldn't be deterred.

"Duane, give your cousin a kiss."

Carolyn was instructed not to move. Feeling trapped, she cringed. Instead of looking at Duane she concentrated on the ball he was still holding in his hand. He placed one knee on the step and leaned forward. She felt his wet kiss on her cheek, heard the camera snap, Aunt Mabel saying, "Weren't they cute?" and it was over.

As they piled happily into their car Carolyn wiped the kiss off her face with the back of her hand. Doug came forward and put his arm around her shoulders. He squeezed her neck in a sort of a hug before he skipped away.

With relief she watched Uncle Homer back the car out of the driveway. He drove slowly down the road, afraid that his tires would throw a stone against the fenders. Carolyn observed them until they reached the curve in the road and disappeared out of sight. A grateful sigh escaped her lips. They were gone. She didn't have to endure any more unwelcome kisses.

Two are stronger than one . . . Ecc. 4:9a

Chapter 7

❦

The Spotted Kitty

To Carolyn each new day was an adventure.

She was little so everything around her, the cows, the tractor and other farm machinery, the two barns and the farm house looked enormous. Even Mommy and Daddy were big. Her brother was big too even though he was only four years older than her.

Everything was bigger than Carolyn except the black and white cat, Spot.

Now Spot was a barn cat. She was not allowed in the house. She lived in the barn where she would catch the mice in the hay loft. She was a good mouser so she never went hungry. She also never missed the nice warm milk that Daddy would squirt into her mouth at milking time. She would wait patiently next to the first cow until Daddy squirted milk at her. She opened her mouth to catch it. She had black whiskers on one side of her face and white ones on the other and always some of the milk would spill over onto them. Sometimes Daddy would miss and the milk would squirt between her ears. When that happened she would shake her head and leave with some of her dignity still intact.

Carolyn loved Spot so much that whenever she held her she would squeeze her too tight. She forgot that Spot didn't enjoy being hugged like that. Spot would scratch her, but Carolyn didn't mind, even though Spot's claws were sharp and they hurt. The only thing that bothered Carolyn was that Spot managed to escape from her and wouldn't come back even when she tried coaxing her.

"Mommy, why doesn't Spot come to me like she does to Daddy? He can always pick her up, but she never lets me. The only time I get to hold her is when Daddy gives her to me, and then she tries to run away."

"I know, Honey. Daddy has a way with animals. They trust him. They know he won't hurt them."

"But I won't hurt her."

"I know you don't mean to, but sometimes you hold her too tightly and she doesn't like it."

"But I wouldn't hold her so tight if she didn't try to get away."

Mommy smiled. She reached out to stroke Carolyn's jet black hair and creamy white face. "If you try to hold her not as tight and let her go when she wants to, then maybe she'll let you hold her more. I know it's hard for you to understand. She's alive. She has feelings and needs. She isn't like one of your dollies. You can squeeze them as tight as you want to and they don't mind. Do you know the difference?"

"Yes, Mommy."

Carolyn did understand what Mommy explained, but she didn't understand why the kitty didn't love her as much as she loved it. Oftentimes Spot would leave the barn and wander through the barnyard, past the brook and into the meadow. She would be gone for hours, but somehow she always knew when it was milking time. She would show up on time for Daddy to squirt milk into her mouth.

One day Carolyn watched Spot leave the barn and make her way delicately through the tall grass. She wondered where Spot went day after day so she decided to follow her.

Spot was stalking something. Fascinated, Carolyn waited with baited breath, but Spot didn't do anything more than wiggle her ears while her tail swished behind her. Carolyn tried to see what it was that Spot was so interested in, but the grass was too tall.

Carolyn decided that it would be a wonderful idea to follow Spot the next time she saw the cat roam away. She planned to try again. Maybe then she could discover the secret.

The next day dawned warm and bright. After breakfast Carolyn went outside to play. She enjoyed watching the dew on the grass melt away when the sun hit it. She smelled the flowers that were in bloom and touched the buds of the ones that weren't.

She was happy as she made her way down to the barn where Spot lived.

She found her in the hay loft. Carolyn squatted down to stroke her soft fur so full of black and white spots. The scratch on the back of her hand was still fresh from yesterday.

"I wonder why you let Daddy pick you up without scratching him. Mommy says it's because he's gentle with you and I hug you too tight, but I try not to.

Mommy says that I can't squeeze you as tight as I do my dollies."

Spot lay down on her side and began to purr. Carolyn was so happy that she had made her purr that she tried to pick her up to hug her. Spot managed to escape without incident.

Carolyn didn't mind too much. She followed the cat down the ramp from the hay loft and into the tall grass. Spot was intent on her journey and Carolyn thought that this was a good time to find out the secret to where Spot went whenever she left the barnyard.

The grass was so tall that only the top of Carolyn's black hair showed as she walked through it. Spot easily picked her way over the brook. Carolyn was certain that she could step on the same rocks so she wouldn't get her feet wet either. She smiled in eager anticipation as she watched where Spot went up the other side of the embankment.

"Carolyn, Carolyn," came Mommy's voice. "Where are you going?"

"I'm going to follow Spot, Mommy." She had to shout to make Mommy hear.

"Come back to the house, Carolyn, you might get lost."

Carolyn turned around. She could see Mommy, but she seemed to be a great distance away.

"Don't worry, Mommy, Spot will bring me home."

"Honey, you might not be able to keep up with Spot. She goes far sometimes and you might get hurt. Better to stay near the house and wait for Spot to come back instead of trying to follow her."

Carolyn knew she couldn't make Mommy understand why she wanted to follow Spot. Mommy would say she knew what was best for her. She looked for Spot, but the cat had already disappeared.

When she reached the house Mommy met her in the yard and gave her a big hug.

"That's my good girl," Mommy told her. "I'm glad I saw you before you went any further. I was afraid you might get lost following Spot. Your little legs can't keep up with her, you know. Promise Mommy that you won't ever try to follow her again, Carolyn."

Carolyn looked up at her mommy. She seemed so tall and very wise. Carolyn could smell fresh baked cookies on Mommy's dress. It made her feel safe. "Okay, Mommy," Carolyn said. "But I know Spot would have brought me home."

"Honey, you can't depend on that. You have to remember that if you wander away from home you might run into trouble. You could get hurt, fall down the well or fall into the brook and drown. You could get so far away from home that you would be too tired to continue so you would sit down on the ground and rest and then you would loose sight of Spot. We might not be able to find you, then. Do you understand?"

Carolyn realized the truth in what Mommy said. She was glad now that she hadn't followed Spot any further. She hugged Mommy's legs as tight as she could. "I'm sorry Mommy," she said. Mommy didn't try to escape. She hugged her right back.

Carolyn might never know the secret of where Spot went, but then Spot would never know the protection and love that only mommies can give.

Children, Obey your parents . . .
Ephesians 6:1a

Chapter 8

In A Strange Place

Douglas needed to have his tonsils out. The doctor didn't want to wait any longer, so Mommy and Daddy agreed to set up an appointment for him at the local hospital in Burlington.

Since Daddy didn't have anyone else to run the farm or do the milking while Dougie was in the hospital, Mommy decided that she and Carolyn would stay with her parents. That way she could leave Carolyn with them during the day, walk to the hospital, which was only a few blocks from their apartment, to be with Doug, then walk back in the evening.

Daddy would have to manage alone.

On Sunday he drove them down. Dougie was very quiet in the back seat. He was bundled up in blankets to keep him warm, his head was on a pillow. His eyes were closed as if he were sleeping.

Carolyn sat in the front seat on Mommy's lap. She

was happy that they were in the car. She loved looking out the window.

Daddy drove to the hospital first. They registered Doug and left him there in the care of the doctors and nurses. Then, they drove to Mommy's parents. Daddy carried Mommy's black suitcase up the stairs to their apartment. Mommy and Carolyn followed.

Daddy stayed only a few minutes. He wanted to go back to the hospital to stay with Doug for as long as he could.

When he left, Carolyn ran to the window. She watched him drive away, but Mommy had promised her that he would be back soon.

The afternoon wore on, but Daddy didn't come back. It got dark. After awhile Mommy put sheets on the day bed in the living room. Her mother brought two extra pillows.

"I wish I had an extra bed for you to sleep on. I hope that you will be comfortable with Carolyn next to you."

"I'm sure that we will be, Ma. Thanks for taking us in."

"Why, what kind of a mother would I be if I didn't help out as much as I could. I only wish I could do more."

Carolyn slept all night in the crook of Mommy's arm. When she woke up Mommy dressed her. They ate breakfast at the small kitchen table.

When Mommy put on her coat Carolyn expected to see Daddy, but instead Mommy hugged her tight, kissed her and told her to be a good girl. She opened the door and disappeared down the stairway, through the door at the bottom and out onto the street.

"Wave good bye to Mommy," the old man with white

hair told her, but she didn't want Mommy to leave. Instead of waving she began to cry.

Her grandmother picked her up. Carolyn struggled against her, but she brought her over to a rocking chair. She sat down with Carolyn on her lap.

Carolyn cried for a long time. Exhausted, she finally put her thumb in her mouth to suck it. Every once in a while a long sob escaped from her, but other than that she was quiet.

The long day passed. It was beginning to get dark when the door opened.

Mommy!

Carolyn scooted away from her grandparents and into Mommy's arms.

"Pearl, I was starting to get worried. I thought something had happened."

"I'm sorry, Ma. Doug was in so much pain it was hard to leave him. I waited until it began to get dark, then I had to hurry through the streets to reach here before nightfall."

"How did the operation go?"

"Everything was fine. The doctor said he should be much better this winter than he was last year."

"You look exhausted."

"I am," Mommy said. She sat down in the chair without even taking her coat off.

That night Carolyn didn't leave Mommy's side. She ate supper sitting on her lap.

When Mommy began to make up the day bed again Carolyn knew that they were spending another night in this strange place. How she hated it! Curled against Mommy she felt safe. Finally, she fell asleep.

The next morning when Mommy was ready to leave Carolyn grabbed her around the leg and wouldn't let go.

"Carolyn, honey, I have to leave. I'm going to walk to the hospital to visit Dougie."

Carolyn began to cry. "Pa, please," Mommy begged.

The white haired old man came and gently pried Carolyn loose. He held her while Mommy hurried down the stairs. When she reached the bottom Carolyn began to cry louder.

This time Carolyn ran from her grandparents. Each time they came near her she would scream, "I want my Mommy." Finally, they decided to leave her alone in the living room while they stayed in the kitchen.

Every so often her grandmother would ask her grandfather if he could see Carolyn. "What is she doing?"

"She's leaning against the day bed, poor little, lost soul," he would say, or "She's watching out the window for her mother."

At last the kindly old gentleman could bear it no longer. "Carolyn," he said, from a respectful distance, "I'm going out to get your Mommy."

Carolyn was excited. He put on his coat and opened the door. She heard him going down the stairs. The bottom door slammed, then he was on the street, but he wasn't headed in the same direction that Mommy had taken.

Presently, he came back. Carolyn ran to the door to see Mommy, but all he had brought back was an ice cream cone.

"I couldn't find your Mommy," he said, "so I brought you this instead."

Carolyn was so angry, she felt so betrayed, that she picked up a shoe and threw it at him. He ducked just in time. It thudded against the door behind his head.

She ran into the living room, wanting nothing from

him. He tried to give her the ice cream, but she refused to take it. She leaned against the day bed watching him, crying in frustration, her hands behind her back.

"What are we going to do? It's starting to melt."

"I will leave it here." He placed it on the corner of the kerosene stove. Since it was a warm day the stove wasn't on.

"Carolyn, here is your ice cream when you want it." Then he went back into the kitchen with his wife.

Carolyn knew they were watching what she was doing, peeking at her around the corner. She could see them as well as they could see her. She wasn't being fooled. She could hear them talking about her in hushed tones.

She stopped crying. The ice cream was dripping down the side of the cone. She missed Mommy and Daddy, the cows, Spot and Betty. She missed her own bed, her toys and Dougie.

She took a step toward the ice cream. She heard her grandfather say, "She's going for it," so she turned away from it stubbornly.

She went back to her silent vigil at the window, but the lure of the ice cream cone was too strong. She decided that she would take only one lick.

She approached it slowly. She knew that her grandparents were watching her from the other room. She took a quick lick, then put the ice cream cone back down on top of the stove. She looked at it. One more lick, she thought. But one led to another. She went over to the window to watch for Mommy while she ate it.

Mommy came back sooner than the night before. Again they slept on the day bed together. The next morning Carolyn clung to Mommy fearfully, but Mommy didn't seem to mind. She continued to reassure Carolyn that she wasn't leaving, but having been deceived by her grandfather the day before she wasn't sure she could believe her.

The bottom door banged. Someone was coming up the stairs. The door opened a crack and there was Daddy's smiling face. Carolyn was so happy to see him she ran to him. He picked her up and swung her high in the air.

Mommy had her black suitcase all packed. Daddy carried it to the car. Carolyn was afraid Mommy was going to leave her again, so she held tightly onto Mommy's hand. But when Mommy left Carolyn went too.

Dougie was laying down in the back seat. He didn't look too well, but he seemed glad to see her.

"Let's go home," Daddy said.

Let us hold fast to hope . . . Hebrews 10:23a

Chapter 9

Birthday Time

Carolyn and Douglas were both born in November. Doug was born on the 7th and Carolyn was born on the 30th.

On his 7th birthday, when Carolyn was almost 3, Mommy began the day by skimming cream off the top of the morning's milk. She was going to make ice cream.

She used an egg beater with a red crank handle to beat the ingredients together until her arm was too tired to continue. Then Daddy took over. When the ice cream became smooth and thick Mommy put it in the freezer. Then she baked a birthday cake.

When Carolyn woke up from her afternoon nap Mommy was icing the cake. Carolyn stood on a chair, her elbows on the kitchen table. Mommy took a big spoon, swirled it around in a bowl and took out a spoonful of chocolate frosting. Plop, onto the cake it went.

Then, with a knife, Mommy very artfully frosted the sides of the two layer cake.

Carolyn could smell the sweet chocolate. She begged Mommy for a taste of it.

"When I'm finished you can have the bowl to clean out," Mommy said.

Carolyn waited impatiently. It seemed like Mommy was scraping the bottom and sides of the bowl until there wouldn't be enough left for Carolyn.

"Mommy," she said. "Don't do any more. Leave some for me."

"Ok, honey, you can have the rest of it. I'm sorry."

Mommy gave her the green bowl and a spoon. The frosting was creamy and rich. It tasted like fudge and it melted in her mouth.

Mommy brought the cake into the pantry where she placed seven white candles on it in a circle. Then she hid it. Carolyn knew that it was Dougie's birthday, but since she didn't remember what his birthday was like the year before she was totally unprepared for what this event meant.

Dougie hopped off the bus. He bounced his way up the path to the cement steps and into the wood-shed.

When he entered the kitchen he smelled the delicious aroma from the birthday cake. He smiled at Mommy who was trying to look like she didn't have a secret hiding in the pantry.

It was Dougie's job every night to bring in the wood for the cook stove. He checked the woodbox before he went back out into the wood shed. He brought in his first armful of wood, then some kindling.

The woodbox wasn't nearly as empty as normal because Daddy had brought in an armful of wood before he went down to the barn for the 3:00 milking. He didn't usually do it, because it was Doug's responsibility, but today was a special day.

Doug wiped the pieces of bark and wood off the front of his coat and sleeves before he hung it up on the hook behind the hall door.

Daddy finished the milking a little early. For supper Mommy had made Doug's favorite, chicken with stuffing and all the fixings, even though it wasn't Sunday.

After they finished the meal, Mommy went into the pantry. When she came out she was carrying the cake and singing *Happy Birthday*. She placed it in front of Doug who took a big lung full of air and blew out the candles. Mommy and Daddy clapped.

Doug got the first piece of cake and Carolyn got the second, with a scoop of the soft ice cream. It was delicious, but Carolyn was beginning to realize that she wasn't the center of attention tonight, but that Doug was. She always was served first. She wondered why Dougie was getting everything first tonight, why Mommy and Daddy were paying him more attention than she was receiving. It didn't make sense. She was the baby.

Then it happened. Daddy went into the back room and came out with an armful of presents. He placed them all on the table in front of Doug.

Enraged, Carolyn started to cry. She couldn't understand why Dougie got presents and she didn't. Mommy tried to soothe her by telling her that in three weeks it would be her birthday. Then it would be her turn to have a cake and presents like Dougie, but it didn't matter. Carolyn wanted a present now.

Carolyn continued to cry. She wanted a new toy. A shiny red tractor like Dougie got. She wanted his new toy.

"I want that, I want that." She stamped her feet angrily.

Dougie hurried through opening his presents while Carolyn continued to scream. When he was finished Daddy helped him bring his new toys and clothes into his bedroom. Mommy threw away the wrapping paper while she tried to calm Carolyn down.

"Now, Carolyn, that is enough. This is Doug's birthday. When it's your birthday then it will be your turn for presents."

But Carolyn could not be pacified. Dougie had gotten presents and she had not. It wasn't fair.

Her throat was sore from crying. She was very tired. Mommy got her ready for bed, then she lay her down in her crib.

Carolyn let out one last sob, a long, gulping sound that wrenched Mommy's heart. Then she began to suck her thumb. Soon she was fast asleep.

When Mommy checked on her later a tear drop still lingered on one of her long, dark lashes.

For I am jealous over you . . .
2 Corinthians 11:2a

Chapter 10

Surprise In the Hayloft

Carolyn was playing outside when it started to snow. The big white flakes seemed to float down from the sky. She opened her mouth wide, lifting it up in an effort to catch the elusive flakes. One landed on her tongue and melted immediately. It was cold, but otherwise quite tasteless. The flakes continued to drift slowly down, each different from all the others.

"Daddy, Daddy," Carolyn cried. "Look, it's snowing."

"I can see that," he replied curtly. Puzzled, Carolyn asked why he didn't like the snow.

"I like it fine, baby. But snow is more fun for children than for grown ups." He touched her head before continuing on his path toward the house.

Additional storms came and went, some fell swiftly to the ground, driven by icy cold winds that howled. By Christmas the snow began to accumulate at an alarming rate.

By February the hard packed snow was several

feet high. Daddy fed the cows from the supply of hay that he had harvested during the summer from his fields and Dr. Devereaux's. The hay loft still had plenty of feed to last through the winter. He wasn't worried about running out like he had in years past.

The cow barn wasn't heated, but it was warm from the body heat the cows gave off. Mommy opened the door that separated the milk room from the main barn. The sweet, dusty odor greeted Carolyn on the threshold. Cheerfully, she hopped down the cement steps: one, two, three into the barn.

The cows stood like solders in two lines, locked in place by the iron stanchions. When they are unlocked the cow leaves the barn. None of the cows minded being in such a predicament. In fact, they felt very secure. Each cow knew exactly where her place in the barn was and welcomed the familiarity of it. It was feeding time so the barn was noisy with their loud mooing.

Mommy and Carolyn were here to help Daddy feed them. Mommy's job was to scoop an equal measure of grain from the burlap bag and place it in front of each cow. There were thirty head, fifteen on each side, and a bag of grain with a scoop in it on each side too. Once a day the cows got fed the grain, but twice a day they were fed hay from the loft. In the morning Mommy helped, but in the afternoon after school while Mommy was busy making supper, Dougie helped with the chores.

Carolyn waited while Mommy carefully measured the grain, then she skipped ahead to where the first cow stood. Mommy poured the feed on the floor in front of the cow who immediately began to lap it up with her tongue. The cow next door stretched her long, thick tongue out trying to reach her neighbor's grain, too. When Mommy returned with the scoop of grain for the next cow the closest one to her tried the same trick, with the same results. The stanchions were spaced far enough apart to keep the creatures from infringing on each other, but that didn't mean that they didn't try every morning to steal from their neighbor's feed. Worried that each cow wouldn't get her proper share, Carolyn grabbed a handful of grain and held it under the next cow's mouth.

The cow's tongue was rough as it licked Carolyn's hand. When Mommy arrived Carolyn moved down the row. Mommy put a little extra grain in Carolyn's hand from the scoop. Finally, Carolyn reached the last cow. It was a pale golden color and Daddy had named her Carol. She was Carolyn's special cow, named for her.

While Mommy went to feed the other animals on the opposite side, Carolyn stayed with her cow. She rubbed between her ears while she ate the grain. There were always large flakes, like dandruff, on the cows' heads.

When Carol was done eating she had bits of grain stuck all over her wet nose. She blew and Carolyn got sprayed. Then the cow took a drink of water from the basin hooked to the right side of the stanchion.

Daddy came down the ladder from the hay loft and began to pitch hay in front of the cows from the pile at the bottom of the hay chute. The musty smelling hay with chafe floating through the air made Carolyn sneeze.

There were two chutes, one on both sides of the barn. Usually the three cows closest to the pile of hay would stretch their necks and reach out with their course tongues to capture as much of it as they could while the ones farthest away mooed loud, plaintive bellows, each wanting a share in the bounty after their grain was gone.

Carolyn went to the pile and pulled out some of the strands. They were stiff. She went over to her cow and began to feed her. Carol pulled at the offering, her mouth working at getting them out of Carolyn's tight grasp. Feeling sorry for Carol's neighbor, Carolyn returned with two handfuls of hay. She held out a hand to each of them.

Soon all the animals were fed. The bawling stopped as the last cow received her portion. Mommy returned to the house and her own chores, but Carolyn stayed with Daddy. It was comforting in the barn watching the cows chew their cuds.

Daddy spread fresh shavings from the silo under the cows so that when they laid down it would be warm and clean for them. The silo door was open so Carolyn went in to walk all the way around it. It was a circle with a very high roof. When she yelled it echoed. It was colder than the barn because it was closed off from it by a very thick wooden door, unless Daddy was working in it, then the door remained open.

When Daddy was finished he told Carolyn he had a surprise to show her. "It's up in the hay loft," he said. His hazel colored eyes twinkled as he smiled at her.

"What is it, Daddy," Carolyn asked. But Daddy wouldn't tell her.

She began to climb the steep ladder to the hay loft. Daddy was right behind her, his protective arms shielding her from an accidental fall from the ladder, his breath warm on her neck. On the top step he pushed open the door, picked her up and swung her into the loft.

"What is it, Daddy?" she asked again with mounting excitement.

"Shh," Daddy said. "See, the cat knows. She followed us up when we came, but we won't let her stay here." He picked Spot up and placed her outside on the ramp that led from the barnyard to the loft. She glanced back at him disdainfully before raising her tail and prancing off. Her little paw prints marked the freshly fallen snow. Then Daddy closed the door so she could not come back in.

Carolyn was puzzled. "Why can't Spot stay? She's always in the hay loft."

"Not any more. Not for awhile, anyway."

Daddy took the pitch fork down from the beam. Gently, cautiously he raised a small section of hay. Inside there was a little mouse family. Daddy reached in and picked one of the babies up. "Hold out your hands, Carolyn. Cup them together like this."

The mouse was pink with only a few fuzzy hairs. Its eyes were closed tight, just like kittens or puppies when they are first born. Carolyn did what Daddy told her. The baby mouse was placed in her cupped palms. It was smaller than her hand.

"I found them this morning when I was pitching down the hay. If I let Spot up here she will kill them all and eat them. That's why I'm going to protect them until they are old enough to fend for themselves."

Cupped in her hand the tiny rodent did look very defenseless. She stroked its back with her finger. It was soft and warm. A long time from now when Carolyn was grown she would probably be afraid of mice, just like Mommy. But on this day she didn't know that fear. Today she had trusted her father.

> *Trust the Lord with all your heart. Lean not to your own understanding. In all your ways acknowledge him and he will direct your path.*
> Proverbs 3:5-6

Chapter 11

❦

The Upstairs

The sun was shining, the snow was melting and Mommy was doing her spring cleaning.

The house had been torn apart for a week. When Mommy cleaned a room she moved all the furniture to the middle of it before she began. She cleaned everything, every square inch of the floor, walls, windows, furniture and ceiling. Every picture, doily, and curtain was washed.

She systematically went through each room, one room a day. In the bedrooms the mattresses and box springs got flipped. In the pantry each cupboard and every dish was washed. Then she put down new cupboard paper with a rose print along the front edge. "Now doesn't that look pretty?" Mommy said. And it did.

Carolyn didn't like things being torn up. She was relieved when nighttime came so the room could be returned to normal. Finally, the only part of the house left was the upstairs.

"Carolyn," Mommy said, "I am going upstairs to clean today."

Carolyn didn't understand what Mommy meant.

"Do you remember last year when you went upstairs with me?"

Carolyn shook her head no.

Mommy gathered together the Hoover vacuum, dust cloth, furniture polish, pail, sponge and other necessities. "We open this door right here in the living room. Remember?"

Carolyn was amazed that a door in a room she played in every day opened into a hall with a beautiful stairway. She held onto the bannister as she climbed the first five steps. Then there was a landing where she turned right to continue on up another eight steps until she reached the top.

Now, the upstairs was never used, but that didn't mean that it was empty. Each of the three bedrooms were completely furnished with antique furniture. Only one room was heated from the stovepipe connected to the kerosene stove in the living room. That was the room that someday, when he was a bigger boy, Doug would move into. Then Carolyn would no longer sleep in the same room with Mommy and Daddy, but she would have Doug's old bedroom, off from theirs.

But for right now Carolyn didn't know any of that. Mommy and Daddy knew, for they had discussed it many times. But Carolyn didn't need to know yet because she lived her life only in the present. Tomorrow was a far off time. She had no concept of next year or two years from now. Mommy and Daddy were wise enough to understand that they didn't need to share their plans for change until just before the event was to take place.

"Come in here with me, Carolyn," Mommy called

to her. She was afraid Carolyn might fall over the banister.

It was a large square room with a four poster bed in it, completely made as if it were waiting for an occupant to pull down the covers that night.

Mommy, however, didn't leave it that way. The first thing she did was strip the bed, then she flipped the mattress over. There were dead flies all over the gray painted wide plank floor boards. Carolyn walked carefully into the room, afraid to step on any. She saw a beautiful oak rocking chair. It was very high, but she managed to climb into it. When she began to rock, though, she could hear the rockers crunch the dead flies. It gave her the willies so she climbed down. Next she walked over to one of the wide windows. On the windowsills more flies lay dead, but a few were buzzing listlessly around the window pane.

"Mommy, why are some of these flies dead and the others aren't?"

"They come back to life in the springtime," Mommy said as if she believed it herself.

Sensing Carolyn's dismay, Mommy used the hose on her vacuum cleaner to suck up all the pests, dead or alive. Once they were gone Carolyn looked beyond the windows to what was outside. She had a beautiful view of the strawberry hill. Comforted by the familiar sight she began to explore the rest of the upstairs.

A connecting closet went from the big front room to another room of equal size. This was where the round stovepipe in the living room disappeared to. This room was warm enough so that Carolyn was able to take off the sweater Mommy had insisted she wear. It wasn't cool like the other rooms up here.

She opened a little built-in cupboard. To her surprise there were three shelves in it. Mommy came into the room with her vacuum.

"Mommy, look at this."

Mommy smiled her knowing smile. "Do you know what that use to be?"

"No, Mommy, what?"

"When this part of the house was first built that was where the stairs came up. They were very steep and narrow with a door on each end, which also made them very dark. I have an identical shelf like that in my bedroom closet except it doesn't have a door on it. A few years ago the people who owned this house before we bought it decided to tear down the old outhouse. They put in new plumbing and made our bathroom. That's when they changed this part of the house. Before, at the bottom of where the stairs are now, there were two huge fireplaces, back to back. They took those out, which opened up that space, and rerouted the stairs."

Mommy pulled the curtains down from the double windows. Curiously, Carolyn went over to peer out. To her amazement she could see the woodshed door and the kitchen window as well as the front lawn where she and Dougie always played. And there, laying on the warm cement step, was Betty. Carolyn felt so much better. This was beginning to be fun.

There was only one more bedroom to explore. That was a small one with a slanted ceiling. It didn't take Mommy any time at all to clean it. While she did, Carolyn walked down a long hallway. She had to bend her head because it also had the slanted ceiling. At the end of it was a small window. Under it was a trunk.

Mommy saw Carolyn trying to open the domed lid on the trunk. It was very heavy.

"Carolyn, don't lift that lid in case it falls back on you. I'll help you in a minute."

When Mommy opened it a strong smell of moth balls and old wood greeted Carolyn's nose rather unpleasantly. Inside the trunk were wondrous things. There was an old quilt with beautiful mint green squares and bright red triangles that were matched and arranged neatly into a star.

"A dear friend helped me make that when your father and I first moved here," Mommy explained to Carolyn, wistfully. "She's gone to heaven now, and this is all I have left to remember her by. That's why I keep it in here instead of on my bed like I use to. I don't want it to get worn out."

Under that was a carefully wrapped picture of Mommy and Daddy. He, sitting in a chair, without glasses and with more hair. She stood next to him in a blue suit, wearing a pert hat with a small veil on the side of her head, and carrying a bouquet of flowers. Her free hand rested lightly on his shoulder. They were smiling into the camera.

"That's my wedding picture," Mommy told her. "We had it taken about a week after we were married. We both wore the same clothes we were married in. Fortunately, my flowers hadn't died yet." Mommy laughed, remembering.

"Why didn't you get married in a white wedding dress, Mommy?"

"Because it was during the depression and we didn't have much money. We almost didn't have a picture taken at all, but my best friend insisted. She told me she would pay for it as her wedding gift to us. I wore a blue suit because there is an old saying that goes, 'if you get married in blue you'll always be true.'"

Carolyn reached into the deeper recesses of the

trunk. She touched something soft and furry. She drew back, suddenly afraid.

"What is it, honey?"

Mommy looked into the trunk, then she pulled out a white muff. She showed it to Carolyn who scooted back away from it. As long as Mommy held it Carolyn didn't go near her.

"Look, you put your hands in each side, like this, to keep them warm. Ladies use to place them on their laps when they went for buggy rides. Touch it, it won't hurt you."

Carolyn shook her head. Her blue eyes were wide with fright.

"What are you afraid of? It can't hurt you. It's soft like your kitty."

But it wasn't a kitty. It wasn't alive. It was unknown.

"I'll put it away, back into the trunk." Mommy repacked the trunk, then closed the lid. She covered it with a flowered cotton percale sheet that was made for it. It fitted over the dome top and was gathered at the sides.

Mommy took Carolyn by the hand and together they walked back down the hall toward the stairs. Mommy left the dirty linen, the vacuum and the household cleaners behind to help Carolyn reach the bottom of the slippery varnished stairs safely. She would return for it later when Carolyn was taking her nap.

Mommy closed the door in the living room. The stairs were no longer visible. Carolyn was relieved to be back in the familiar environment that she was used to.

I am with you always . . . Matthew 28:26a

Chapter 12

The Easter Bunny

Mommy and Daddy took Doug and Carolyn shopping for their new Easter outfits. They went all the way down to J.C. Penney's on Church Street in Burlington, the biggest city in Vermont. It was twenty-five miles from their farm.

Daddy circled Church Street once, but couldn't find an empty parking space so he parked along a side street. They bailed out of the car. It wasn't every day they went shopping.

Carolyn was excited. She had a hard time waiting for Daddy to find the exact change for the meter. It was a short walk to the corner where the store was located. It was large with three double glass doors on the front. Daddy opened the first one they came to. He and Dougie stepped aside to let Carolyn and Mommy to go in first.

There weren't a lot of people in the store. It was still too early in the morning.

Mommy brought Carolyn over to the Easter

dresses. They picked a pink one with a full skirt. Carolyn did so love to twirl around and around, watching the skirt billow out. Mommy knew she would like this one.

Next they went to the shoe department. Carolyn was instructed to sit down on one of the red chairs that were all connected together. She was afraid to sit next to the lady with the hat so she sat at the end.

A man came up to help them. Mommy asked for a pair of white shoes for Carolyn. The man sat down on a stool in front of her. He tried to pick up her leg, but she tightened it so he couldn't lift it.

Daddy stood with his hands in his pockets, jiggling the change he kept there. "Carolyn, let the man measure your foot."

So that was what he was doing. Carolyn let him bring her foot up to measure it against a long, metal object. Her foot was very small compared to it.

While he went into a back room Carolyn watched how the other salesman was fitting a new shoe onto the stranger's foot who sat in the chair on the other side of the empty one. She saw him take the new shoe off, place her old one back on and lace it up for her. Carolyn decided to sit back and relax. This was going to be fun.

The young salesman returned with two boxes. He took Carolyn's foot and gently fit the new shoe on. Daddy had her stand up to put her full weight on it while the salesman pushed against the end where her toes were.

"It's a little tight," he told Mommy. "Do you want to try a half size bigger?"

"Better too big than too small," Mommy said. The salesman agreed.

The bigger shoe felt more comfortable. The young

man took the shoe off, but he didn't pick up Carolyn's old shoe. He just got up and went over to the cash register. Mommy paid him. It was time to leave.

"Come on, Carolyn, let's go."

"I can't go yet. He hasn't put my shoe on."

Dougie was embarrassed. Daddy told her to put it on herself, but she said no, the man had to do it for her.

By this time the young salesman was waiting on another customer, but he left her to come back to Carolyn. He picked her foot up and placed it into her own shoe, then laced it up.

Mommy said thank you very much, and they went to the boy's department.

Bored, Carolyn wandered a little ways off. There was a lovely mannequin with long brown hair, posed in a beautiful spring dress. Carolyn paused to study her. She was very tall and slender. Her fingers were stiff and she stared straight ahead. She was up on a platform so Carolyn climbed on it for a closer look.

Mommy saw her. She came over to her quickly and told her to come down. Carolyn did, but the salesman said that it was alright, most children were fascinated by mannequins.

"She isn't hurting anything. You can leave her there."

Mommy said, "You can stay, but don't get up on that platform. I don't want you to knock the mannequin down."

"Isn't she pretty, Mommy?"

Mommy smiled indulgently. "Be a good girl," she cautioned before returning to Daddy and Doug.

Carolyn began to talk to the mannequin like she did with her dolls. She didn't notice the amused looks she received from other costumers. Her eyes were totally concentrated on the beautiful lady who didn't talk.

Carolyn told her all about her animals and the farm. She touched her waxed hand. She gazed at the dark eyes under the thin outline of perfect eyebrows, she studied the brown hair tucked under the pert hat balanced on the side of her head. All the while she talked the lady just stood there, smiling her calm, unnatural smile.

Mommy and Daddy finished their purchases and then it was time to go home. Mommy came for Carolyn and took her hand.

"I have to go now," she told the mannequin. "Goodbye." The tall lady seemed sad to see Carolyn leave.

The next day was Easter Sunday. Carolyn knew that the Easter bunny was suppose to bring an Easter basket filled with candy. She heard that the bunny hid colored eggs. That was very confusing because she knew that eggs came from chickens, not bunnies. Mommy told her it was one of the mysteries of life that she would understand when she got older.

That night Mommy heard Carolyn's prayers as she knelt by her bed. When she was all tucked in Mommy pushed a ladder-back chair up against the bed on one side so that if Carolyn rolled too close to the edge of the bed she wouldn't fall out. The other side of the bed was against the wall.

Carolyn fell fast asleep sucking her thumb and twirling her hair. When she woke it was dark.

"Mommy, I'm thirsty. Mommmmmy."

Mommy answered from her bed. Carolyn could hear her fumbling for her slippers in the dark. Mommy turned the light on in the bathroom.

"I don't like the water from there. I want a glass of water from the kitchen."

Mommy went out to the kitchen. Carolyn's eyes

were becoming accustomed to the dim light. A dark shape was perched on her chair. She looked at it more closely.

Mommy came back with a full glass. Carolyn took a sip of water and handed the glass back to Mommy.

"What's this, Mommy?" Carolyn asked as her hand brushed something on the chair. She pulled it closer to the light.

It was a big, stuffed yellow and white bunny. Its arms curved out in a hug. Carolyn grabbed it to her and hugged it. The rabbit's arms seemed to fit perfectly around her neck as though he were returning her hug.

"Is it mine?" she asked in wonderment.

"Yes." She could hear Mommy's smile in the dark. "The Easter Bunny must have left it for you. It was on the chair next to your bed."

"Can I sleep with it?"

"If it will fit in your bed along with all your dolls." Mommy helped her get settled in before she went back out into the cold kitchen to empty the nearly full glass of water.

In the morning light Carolyn examined her Easter Bunny more minutely. It had long ears, a hard plastic nose and mouth with whiskers set into it, and a small round tail. It also had a plaid vest and a bow-tie at the front of his neck.

Carolyn, with Doug's prompting, searched for the famed Easter basket, but she couldn't find it. Finally she gave up and let Dougie find both of them.

After church they were going to Aunt Dorrie's house for dinner. They loaded the trunk with the food that Mommy had cooked the day before, plus Carolyn's new bunny.

Carolyn worried about Bunny being in the trunk.

She asked Mommy if she was sure that Bunny would be able to breath alright back there. Mommy kept reassuring her that he could.

When they finally reached Aunt Dorrie's house Carolyn rushed to the back of the car. Daddy opened the trunk and there was Bunny, safe and sound.

Aunt Dorrie came out to greet them. She raved over each one of Mommy's homemade pies as they were carried into the house.

"I swear, Pearl, each one looks better than the last. I can't wait to get through dinner just so I can have dessert. They all look so good I don't know which one I'll try."

"Well, you'll just have to try them all, Dorrie."

"Oh, I couldn't do that. Then your brother would divorce me for getting fat." They laughed together as they went into the house.

Carolyn was too little to reach into the trunk for Bunny. She tried, but her fingers just didn't make it all the way over to where he lay on his back. Gary, one of Aunt Dorrie's sons, reached in and grabbed Bunny by one arm. He handed the stuffed animal to Carolyn. But instead of saying thank you, Carolyn was indignant.

"If you grab him by his arm like that you're going to hurt him," she said in Mommy's grown up stern voice.

Gary didn't seem to care. His eyes twinkled in merriment at his little cousin as he closed the lid on Daddy's trunk.

> *When I was a child I spoke and thought and reasoned as a child does. But when I became grown my thoughts grew far beyond those of my childhood, and now I have put away the childish things. In the same way, we can see*

and understand only a little about God now, as if we were peering at his reflection in a poor mirror; but someday we are going to see him in his completeness, face to face. Now all that I know is hazy and blurred, but then I will see everything clearly, just as clearly as God sees into my heart right now. Corinthians 13:11-12

Chapter 13

❦

Mommy

Carolyn and Doug were playing on the kitchen floor with his farm set. There was a red tin barn with a pretend hayloft painted on the side. The front part was open so it was easily accessible to small hands. There were several white railing fences. He had cows, chickens, horses, two pigs, and a rooster. There was a silo, taller than the barn, with a removable top. He also had a tractor and a rake.

Carolyn was upset with the way Doug wasn't letting her set anything up her way. She knocked all the animals down. Then she kicked the barn and silo.

"No, no, no," she screamed while tears rolled down her cheeks.

Douglas jumped to his feet. "Stop it. You're ruining it!"

Mommy was nearby in the pantry. She knew Carolyn was coming down with something. Her eyes were bright, her cheeks were flushed and she had a rash.

"Doug, put the set away for now." Mommy felt Carolyn's forehead. She felt hot.

"Come on, honey. I want to take your temperature." Meekly Carolyn took Mommy's hand.

Mommy timed how long the thermometer was in Carolyn's mouth. When three minutes were up she took it out. She turned the thermometer until she could read it. 103.5! She was concerned that if the fever went any higher Carolyn might have a convulsion. Since they didn't have running hot water, she hurried out to the kitchen for the big tea kettle she kept on top of the cookstove. Carefully she carried the full kettle into the bathroom. She emptied it into the bathtub. Then she added cold water from the faucet.

Carolyn sat in the bathtub while Mommy squeezed water from a wash cloth all over her. She didn't need to use soap since she was only trying to reduce the fever, not give her a bath.

Carolyn sat in a stupor. She felt the water soothe her hot skin, but then she had goosebumps. She was hot and cold at the same time.

Mommy reached for the towel that hung from a roller on the oak medicine cabinet. She wrapped Carolyn in it. When she was dry Mommy dressed her in clean underwear and a nightgown. Then she put her to bed.

A few minutes later Mommy was back. "If you lift your nightie up I'll rub alcohol on your back and legs, honey." It was too great an effort. Mommy helped her with it. Then she gently pulled her t-shirt up.

The alcohol rub felt good. When Mommy was done she covered Carolyn with blankets, then pulled the shades down.

When Carolyn woke from her nap her mouth hurt. She tried to swallow, but that hurt too. Her head was throbbing and her skin felt like it was on fire. She was itchy all over.

Mommy had been listening for Carolyn to awaken. After she raised the shades she went over to look at her daughter.

"How do you feel?" she asked as she sat down on the edge of the bed.

Carolyn told her. Mommy looked inside her mouth. Her tongue was coated white. Then Mommy noticed the bumps on the side of her mouth. She went to get the flashlight and a teaspoon. When she returned she had Carolyn open her mouth again. This time she depressed her tongue with the spoon.

"Say ahhh," Mommy instructed.

The flashlight revealed red spots in Carolyn's mouth and throat. Mommy picked up one of Carolyn's arms. She pushed the flannel sleeve of the nightgown up. Then she examined Carolyn's legs, tummy and back.

"Well, my girl," she said. "It looks to me like you've got the German measles."

Carolyn didn't care what she had. She just knew she was sick. She started to scratch, but Mommy told her not to. She went to the medicine cabinet for the

Calamine lotion. She dabbed it on Carolyn's spots with a cotton ball.

The cool lotion felt comforting against her itchy skin. Mommy brought Carolyn a hot cup of tea. She wanted to make certain that Carolyn would have a good case of the measles the first time around instead of a possible light episode and then a second exposure. Good hot tea would bring the spots out. After she finished it Mommy tucked Carolyn in. Soon she was asleep again.

She slept fitfully through the rest of the day and that night.

The next morning Carolyn's fair skin was peppered with spots. There wasn't an inch of space anywhere that was clear. They were even on her scalp.

Mommy carried her out to the kitchen where it was warmer. She had placed heavy, clean towels on the table. She laid Carolyn on them. She helped her off with her nightie, then she gave her a sponge bath, lightly touching her skin with a cloth dipped in lukewarm water.

Carolyn felt so miserable that she whimpered. Her skin hurt. Her throat was badly swollen. It was almost impossible to swallow.

"I know, honey, I know how much it hurts," Mommy told her over and over while she sponged her off. Then she dabbed soothing Calamine lotion on her itchy spots again. She dressed her in a fresh nightie and put her back to bed.

Whenever Carolyn began to moan Mommy was right there. She repeatedly brought her out to the kitchen for a sponge bath and more lotion. She gave her water to drink and tried to feed her ice cream. She made her drink eggnogs for nourishment.

Mommy sang to her so that she might forget temporarily that she wanted to scratch. She sang *My Wild*

Irish Rose while she rocked her. Carolyn's skin was so hot Mommy could feel it burning her hands through the nightgown.

Day and night Mommy tended to her until Carolyn was better. Her fever was down, the red spots had come to a head the day before and now they were starting to disappear. It was easier to swallow. She ate a little bit of broth.

"Mommy, will you sing to me again?"

Mommy smiled. "Yes, what do you want to hear?"

"*My Wild Irish Rose*?"

Mommy followed the sprinkling of freckles across Carolyn's nose and cheeks with her forefinger. "That's what you are, you know, my little Irish rose, the sweetest flower that grows."

Mommy picked Carolyn up. She carried her to the rocking chair. She was so tired, but tonight she would get a good night's sleep. Her little Irish rose was better. Yes, tonight she would sleep soundly.

> *He shall feed his flock like a shepherd: he shall gather the lambs with his arm, and carry them in his bosom, and shall gently lead those that are with young.* Isaiah 40:11

Chapter 14

The Playmates

Mommy hung up the phone.

"We're going to have company the day after tomorrow," she told Carolyn. "My friend, Jane Royer, and her two little girls are coming over."

Carolyn was very excited. She so seldom had any friends to play with. Even when her cousins came over they were mostly boys. She had only one girl cousin who was two years older than her. The rest were grown ups.

"What are they like, Mommy?"

"They are very nice girls. One is a year older than you and the other is a year younger."

"What are their names?"

"The older one is Toni and the younger is Tammy."

Carolyn could hardly wait. She had such plans for them. She wanted to show them her dolls and her doll house. She dreamed about playing house since that was one game Dougie refused to play with her. If it was a nice day maybe they could play tag out in the yard. She had a little red ball that she liked to throw, but she seldom had anyone to catch it. She would throw the ball and then have to run after it. She wondered if they would play a game of catch with her.

The two days seemed to drag by. Finally it was the morning of the day they were coming. Carolyn went outside to wait for them. Daddy had made Carolyn a swing. The seat was made out of a plank of wood. It was a wide seat, much wider than Carolyn. The rope on each side was a thick braid. Both sides were looped securely over an overhanging tree limb.

Carolyn grabbed the rope. Her backside was against the seat, but in order to hop on she had to push the swing backwards to where the ground was slightly higher. She got on her tip toes and pushed off. When the swing came forward she pulled against the rope and hopped onto the seat.

She loved to swing. Sometimes Dougie would get on it with her. He stood, his feet on either side of her. She would pump with her legs like Daddy taught her and Dougie would push down with his knees. The higher she went the more it tickled her tummy.

Today Doug was in school. Carolyn didn't feel like going high on the swing. She was more interested in listening for the sound of a car coming down the dirt road.

Betty kept her company while she waited. She rubbed the dog's head, especially behind her ears. She scratched Betty's back. Her tail was wagging in satisfied pleasure and adoration.

Suddenly Carolyn heard a car. It was coming slowly down the hill. It pulled into the driveway.

A short, heavyset woman got out of the car along

with two girls. They had long, wavy, dark hair. They looked alike except they weren't the same size.

Betty trotted over to the car, barking at the intruders. Both little girls began to scream. Their mother stood between them and the dog. She ordered Carolyn to hold onto the dog's collar until they could get into the house.

Mommy greeted her company at the door. Carolyn held onto Betty until everyone was safely inside. Then Carolyn went in too.

Mommy had molasses cookies and three glasses of milk on the table. While Carolyn washed her hands Mommy poured tea for herself and Mrs. Royer.

It was like having a tea party, only with real people instead of dolls and the tiny tea service Carolyn pretended with. She listened politely to Mommy and her guest while she munched on the cookies. She watched the two sisters. They were sharing a chair. They each ate two cookies apiece. Carolyn was finished with hers while they were still on their first one. She had never seen anyone eat so slowly before.

After they were done Carolyn asked Mommy if they could go play in her bedroom, but the girls didn't want to. So she brought her dolls out to the kitchen to show them. They took them, but they didn't want to play with Carolyn, only with each other. Mrs. Royer said they were shy.

Carolyn was disappointed, but determined. She asked them if they wanted to go outside to play a game of catch.

Mrs. Royer said they were afraid of the dog.

"Betty won't hurt them, will she Mommy?"

Mommy urged them to go outside. She told them that Betty was very gentle with children.

Carolyn continued to beg, the girls continued to

refuse. Finally, Mrs. Royer decided that since it was such a nice day they should all go outside. Elated, Carolyn jumped from the table.

Mommy and Mrs. Royer stood around while Carolyn tried to play with the girls. She threw the ball at Toni, but instead of catching it she screamed that the dog was coming. She and Tammy ran for the swing. She stood on it, then she pulled her little sister after her. They stood there hanging onto the ropes, the swing swaying gently. Carolyn watched in amazement. She couldn't understand why they were so afraid of Betty.

Mommy called Betty over to her so the girls would climb off the swing. Carolyn got them set up in a triangular circle again. This time she threw the ball at Tammy, who missed it. When she ran after it Betty ran too. Toni screamed that the dog was coming, and both girls were standing on the swing again.

Once more Carolyn managed to coax them down. She even brought Betty over for them to pet, so they could see for themselves how gentle she was, but that was a mistake since they immediately climbed back onto the swing.

Carolyn stood behind them and a little to the side. Betty was right next to the swing. Both girls were screaming frantically, but they didn't really look frightened. They looked like they were enjoying themselves.

Exasperated, Carolyn sat down on the cement steps. She called Betty over. While she held onto the collar the two girls scampered to their mother's side who quickly loaded them into the car before Betty could hinder them. As she backed out of the driveway Carolyn and Betty went over to Mommy.

"Well, that wasn't much fun, was it?" Mommy said. "I didn't know they would be that afraid of a dog, especially a dog as gentle as Betty."

Hearing her name Betty thumped the ground with her tail.

"You look disappointed, honey. I'm sorry it didn't work out for you."

"Mommy, you always say I'm shy, but I don't act like that."

"They might be shy, but more than shyness, they are just plain spoiled. You don't act like that because I have raised you to not act like that. They act like that because it gives them more attention. I was proud of you today, but if I was their mother I wouldn't be proud of the way they had behaved."

Carolyn was glad that Mommy was her mother. She wouldn't like it if Mrs. Royer was. She didn't want to act the way they had acted, although it would be nice to have a little sister.

Carolyn sighed as she returned to her swing. Betty came over and Carolyn's hand caressed her back each time she swung past.

> *The character of even a child can be known by the way he acts—whether what he does is pure and right.* Proverbs 20:11

Chapter 15

Betty and the Mowing Machine

Many years ago, when the first settlers came to Vermont, a man cleared a piece of land by chopping down the trees. He built a log cabin for himself and his family. He planted grass and raised a crop. All around the small clearing were tall trees. For one reason or another, the man eventually left. His cabin fell into ruin, but the work he had done clearing that piece of land endured until it became part of the 250 acre farm that Daddy owned. It was called the upper meadow, accessible only by walking through the forest that surrounded it.

It was a fine sunny day. The cows were feeding in the upper meadow. They took their time coming down to be milked. A few had started down the lane that led across the brook and into the barnyard, but most were still grazing near the stone foundation of the old log cabin.

It was almost 3 o'clock. Daddy went into the milk room and picked up his pails.

With the first rattle of the milk pails Betty headed for the woods to gather up the cows. She was a good cow dog, one of the best. Whenever the cows or even one stubborn cow didn't come, Daddy could count on her to find them and bring them home.

She had become part of the family. Carolyn loved to pet her. Her fur was long and Carolyn's fingers glided over the smooth coat.

Sometimes Dougie would ride on her back. His feet on either side touched the ground. When Carolyn tried it she invariably slid off before Betty could take more than a couple of steps. But she didn't mind really. She liked Betty as a dog. It was Dougie who wanted a horse.

When Betty came home from finding the cows Carolyn was laying on the ground in the front yard under the shade of the maple tree. Betty was panting, her heavy coat was hot. She went over to Carolyn and laiy down beside her.

The warm, lazy days of June melted into July. Soon the hay was tall enough to cut. Daddy fastened the mowing machine onto the right side of his John Deere tractor. The blades were very sharp and they cut with deadly precision.

Betty was part bird dog. She loved nothing better than running in a field of tall grass sniffing out birds nesting there. Whenever Daddy mowed a field Betty would chase the birds that flew up in front of Daddy's tractor. Daddy became use to seeing Betty in the field with him.

The meadow directly behind the house needed mowing. Carolyn watched Daddy from the kitchen window.

The field and rolling meadow were pungent with the smell of new-mown hay. By tomorrow it would be dry enough to rake. After it was raked into furrows Daddy could begin to load the hay onto the wagon with the hayloader. The hay loft was empty now, but soon it would be full again from the summer's crop.

Carolyn worried aloud that Betty was running too close in front of the mowing machine.

"Daddy knows she's there. He'll be careful not to hit her," Mommy said.

Carolyn continued to watch Daddy mow the hay. He was very close to the house now. Even though Mommy said there was nothing to worry about Carolyn felt unsettled with Betty darting about.

Daddy turned to look behind him. Just then a flock of birds flew up in front of the tractor. Betty leaped out in pursuit and the mower cut into her.

Carolyn screamed as Betty fell into the tall grass. The tractor stopped with a jerk and Daddy jumped off.

Dougie, Mommy and Carolyn were all standing at the window watching. Dougie and Carolyn wanted to run outside, but Mommy wouldn't let them. She was afraid. If Betty was badly injured she didn't want them to see her like that.

It seemed like an eternity passed before Daddy picked Betty up and carried her into the kitchen. His face was ashen, his hands were bloody.

Mommy opened the door for him. Daddy felt bad. He blamed himself for the accident. "I didn't see her. I just didn't see her," he said. "One minute she was behind me and the next minute I felt the mowing machine run into her."

"What can I do?" Mommy asked.

"Fill a pan with cold water. Maybe if we make a

compress we can stop the bleeding. Then we can bandage it."

Daddy was very gentle with Betty. She seemed to understand that he hadn't meant to hurt her. Mommy got the Sunday paper that she saved each week to start the fire in the wood stove. She covered a section of the floor with it. Daddy laid Betty down on it. Then he tenderly lifted her hind leg to survey the damage.

It was badly cut. He felt along it as gently as possible. He decided that the bone and tendons hadn't been injured. He and Mommy wrapped cold compresses around the leg until the heaviest bleeding subsided.

That night Betty slept in the kitchen. The next morning she was still laying on her side. She didn't open her eyes unless Carolyn or someone spoke her name, and then they opened only briefly. She looked dead except for the occasional rise and fall of her side.

"Is she going to live, Daddy?"

"I don't know. I hope so."

No one suggested that they call the vet because he was never called in unless one of the cows needed attention, and that was after Daddy tried to tend to the cow first. There wasn't extra money to call the vet for a dog, even if she was a good cow dog and part of the family.

Daddy felt it was his fault that Betty was hurt. Mommy kept saying it was an accident, that it could have happened to anyone. He was as careful as he could be. He hadn't known she would jump right in front of the mowing machine. How could he have prevented her from doing what she loved to do the best, which was to chase birds.

He rubbed the back of his neck and head with his hand. "I should have been more careful," was all he said.

Twice that day Daddy changed the bandages. She whimpered when he touched her leg. She would neither drink water nor eat. Daddy knew that there was nothing more he could do.

The next morning Carolyn came into the kitchen for breakfast. Mommy was picking up the newspapers. Betty was gone.

"Is she dead?" Carolyn asked, fearing the worse.

"No. She's up walking." Mommy answered. "She can only use three legs, but she's a lot better. This morning she drank some water from the dish and then she went over to the door. Daddy let her out."

Carolyn ran to the window to see. Betty was laying in the shade tugging at the bandage on her leg.

Betty continued to pull at the white bandage all day. At supper time Daddy brought her back into the kitchen to change the dressing. When he took the bandage off Betty began to lick the wound.

"That's what she's being wanting to do all day," he said in some amazement. "Why didn't I think of it before. God has given her the ability to heal her own leg by licking it. I'm not going to bandage it up. I'm going to let her tongue heal it."

Daddy was right. In no time at all Betty was running around again, chasing the cows, birds, and the kids.

August was very hot. For more than a week the temperature was in the nineties. It was good haying weather. Daddy was in the fields every day. Betty was too, only this time she didn't come as close to the tractor.

One morning Mommy kept Carolyn and Dougie in the house.

"Why can't we go out to play?"

"Because Betty is real sick, honey. She's out of her head. She didn't know Daddy this morning."

"Where is she?"

"Daddy has her tied up in the tool shed." The tool shed was a three-sided building that was a few yards away from the horse barn. Daddy kept his racks and hayloader there.

"Can we see her, Mommy?"

"I'm afraid not. We'd better stay in the house today until Daddy says it's safe to go out again."

All day long Betty barked and growled. She pulled against the rope and the tool shed shook, but she didn't get loose.

The next morning dawned with less humidity. It was a relief not to have it as hot as it had been.

"It's a beautiful morning," Mommy observed.

"Can we go out to play today?"

Mommy said they could.

"How about Betty?"

"Betty isn't in pain anymore."

Carolyn was glad. She didn't grasp Mommy's meaning, but Douglas did.

"When did she die?" he asked with a quiver in his voice.

"Sometime during the night. Your father is out burying her right now."

"Oh, no," Carolyn wailed.

Mommy held her until she was quiet again.

The Lord gave, and the Lord hath taken away; blessed be the name of the Lord. Job 1:2lb

Chapter 16

Pip and Mim's Vacation

"Whew, I made it just ahead of the storm." Daddy was breathing hard. He had run from the barn to the house, narrowly escaping the downpour.

The thunder rumbled directly overhead and the lightening made zigzag circles in the sky. But Carolyn was safe in the big, white farmhouse with Mommy and Daddy.

Daddy's smile lit up his face. "We got the hay in just on time. For a while there I didn't think we were going to make it."

"Doug did a good job driving the tractor," Mommy said proudly.

"He's getting to be a big help around the farm."

"Imagine the days when you use to put the tractor in low gear, set it in a straight line down a row of hay, hop down from it, and load the hay onto the wagon. If the tractor hit a bump or began to go off course you'd run up to it and turn the wheel before going back to load again. How did you ever manage?"

"It was easier when we had the horses. At least when I pointed them in the right direction they knew enough to go in a straight line."

Daddy wiped his freshly washed face and hands with a clean towel, then he handed it to Dougie to dry off with.

"Except for that blind horse, remember?" Mommy and Daddy laughed. "She was a good work horse, though, I've got to admit, even though she couldn't see a thing."

Daddy sat down in the chrome rocker with the red back and seat pad. Mommy sat down on one of the wooden chairs at the kitchen table.

The wind was beating the rain against the windows. It was getting darker outside. Suddenly the lights went out.

"Well, there goes our electricity. I expect it'll be sometime tomorrow before they locate the line that's down and repair it."

Mommy went over to the sideboard to get a candle. She lit it and placed it in the middle of the table.

"I hope my meat doesn't spoil in the freezer. I'll have to cook it up in the morning if it's unthawed."

The freezer in Mommy's refrigerator was only large enough to hold two or three packages of meat.

"Before it gets too dark I'll go and get the kerosene lantern from the big front room downstairs."

The farmhouse had two big front rooms, one was upstairs above the other.

"I'll get it for you," Daddy said. "Where is it?"

"On the organ." They had an old upright organ in that room. In order for sound to come out of it the person playing had to pump the pedals at the bottom.

No one played it, though, since no one knew how. They kept it because someone had given it to them and it was too heavy to move. Besides, it was pretty and it was just the right size for the wall it was against.

Daddy brought the lantern back into the kitchen. Mommy trimmed the wick, then lit it. It gave off more light than the candle.

"Remember the time that Pa came up here for a vacation the first summer after we moved in? We had a terrible storm that night, too."

Daddy nodded his head.

Carolyn sat down on the floor. She liked the times when Mommy and Daddy weren't too tired to share stories.

"What happened, Mommy?" Carolyn and Dougie begged to hear more.

"Pa was a crackerjack teamster. He could handle even the worst of horses, but he'd always lived in Burlington. He'd never stayed on a farm before. He was deathly afraid of bulls. The only way we got him to come was by telling him that we didn't own any bulls, which was true."

"We moved here in November. The place was a mess. The people who had stayed here before us just rented so they didn't take care of it. When we bought it there was a big, black cookstove in the living room. It took us months to get the house livable, so we hadn't seen too many people during that time and I had never lived that far away from my parents before. That summer they decided to come for a visit, but Pa never learned how to drive a car so my brother, your Uncle Ray, brought them up."

"It was the first vacation they had ever taken. I knew Pa was nervous, but we figured everything would turn out alright. We didn't think anything could go wrong. We didn't own a bull."

Daddy chuckled. Carolyn squirmed excitedly. Her eyes sparkled. She looked over at Dougie who was sprawled on the floor, laying on his belly, his chin cupped in his hands. He was smiling in eager anticipation.

Pip was older than Mim by sixteen years. She was his second wife, his first having died giving childbirth. Carolyn saw them slightly more often than she did Daddy's parents.

Mim and Pip was a slang version, or a more affectionate term than the French Meme and Pepe. Since Mim and Pip weren't from Canada they didn't mind being called that.

Carolyn knew that Mommy had two half brothers that were older than her, but she didn't understand why they were half. They looked like whole people to her. Mommy said that she would understand it when she was older.

Carolyn hated that. She wanted to know now. She didn't want to wait until later.

Uncle Ray was a red faced Irishman. He didn't look anything like Mommy because his mother had been Irish, whereas her mother was French and Scotch. He drove Mim and Pip from where they lived in Burlington to Mommy's house.

When they arrived Mommy made a great fuss over them. Daddy brought their suitcases upstairs to the big front room with the four poster bed. The room was immaculate because Mommy had cleaned it for them.

"Ma took one look at that bed. She said that it would feel odd to sleep in a strange bed after so many years in the same one."

Daddy added, "She was homesick already and they had only just arrived."

"That should have been my first clue as to how the rest of the weekend was going to go." Mommy was sitting in the chair sideways, her right arm was resting on the back of it. She waved her hand, expressively showing her disgust. Daddy chuckled.

"I made Pa an apple pie because he liked them so much. He had a big wedge of cheese with it, remember?"

Daddy nodded. A haze of blue smoke from his cigarette encircled his head.

"Here comes another one," Daddy said looking out the window as the lightening danced. A rumble of far off thunder accompanied it.

"After supper we had a bad storm. Pa was fit to be tied. He kept pacing back and forth. He was already nervous about being on the farm. It was too open for him. When he looked out the window all he could see was pitch black. There were no street lights. He couldn't see a thing."

Pip had a full head of white hair that he parted down the middle. He had blue eyes and he walked with a limp. When he was young he had been a stable boy. One of the horses had kicked him in the hip. From then on that one side didn't grow so he had a short leg when he was an adult.

Mommy continued with the story. "All Ma kept saying was 'calm down, Pet, before you give yourself a heart attack.'"

"After a while the rain stopped and we went to bed. Your father and I were tired, but Pip was all nerved up. He couldn't fall asleep. When he finally did sleep he dreamt of a huge, black bull with horns that were six feet wide. It had red eyes and steam pouring out of its nostrils. He pawed at the ground and tore it up. He heard the bull snorting and bellowing. He felt the house shake as though the bull had run up against the building."

Pip sat straight up in bed. Shivering in his nightshirt he crept over to the window. Timidly he lifted the shade and peered out into the shadowy night. He thought he vaguely made out a shape. It pawed the ground, then charged the house. Wham!

Pip hurried downstairs as fast as he could. "Ray, Pearl, get up. I think there's a bull outside."

"Go back to bed, Pa," Daddy said sleepily. "We already told you we don't own a bull."

"No, really, Ray, I saw it. It's right outside my bedroom window."

Right then the house shook. Daddy was out of bed like a shot. He pulled his pants on over his pajamas, grabbed a flashlight and went outside.

"Be careful, Ray," Mommy called after him.

He was gone only for a minute. When he came back in he told them that there was indeed a bull outside charging the house.

"Pa was right. I think it's Jack Thompson's bull. Distract him while I get the car. I don't want him charging me."

So while Daddy went over to the Thompson's house Mommy and Pip made faces at the bull through the window. They used a flashlight and a candle to keep him distracted while they danced and sang and talked to him.

The bull watched in fascination. He pawed the ground, and when he did they were afraid he would charge right through the window at them, so they separated. Mommy stood in one window and Pip in the other.

The bull was confused. He couldn't make up his mind over which one he should charge at first.

Daddy came back with Jack Thompson right behind him. Mr. Thompson went as close to the raging bull as he dared. He saw the whites of his eyes and he shot him.

"There's no fooling around with a mad bull," he said. "Sorry, Ray. If there is any damage to your house let me know and I'll pay for it. I'll be back tomorrow to pick up the carcass."

"Thanks, Jack," Daddy said.

"I'm just glad no one was hurt. Good night."

One night of quiet excitement was all Pip could take. Early the next morning Pip and Mim were on their way back to Burlington in Uncle Ray's car.

Mommy finished the story. "Before Ma left she said to me, 'I'm sorry, Pearl, but you understand.' I understood, alright. The farm was no place for Pa. What I didn't understand was how Ma could have slept through the whole thing. When she arrived she was so worried about sleeping in a strange bed and yet she slept so soundly that even when Jack Thompson shot the bull right under her bedroom window she didn't wake up."

Baffled, Mommy shook her head from side to side. Daddy chuckled. Dougie and Carolyn laughed.

> *. . . he who watches over you will not slumber.*
> Psalm 121:3b

Chapter 17

Sheila and the Strawberries

Cousin Sheila was here from Connecticut for a visit. She was the daughter of one of Daddy's sisters. She had a job, but every summer on her two week vacation, she came to stay on the farm.

Carolyn didn't particularly like Sheila, even though she was the only cousin that shared Carolyn's coloring. With black hair, blue eyes, and white complexion, they looked like Snow White, or at least Carolyn did. Sheila was too fat to look like Snow White.

The other reason why Carolyn didn't like Sheila was that she insisted on helping Mommy around the house, which meant that she took over the care of Carolyn. While Mommy dusted the living room Sheila brushed out Carolyn's long, thick hair. But she didn't do it gently like Mommy did every morning. Sheila yanked the brush through Carolyn's hair. She pulled at each snarl with heavy hands, tugging until it made tears come into Carolyn's eyes.

"Mommy, please brush my hair."

"I'm brushing your hair, now sit still."

"Mommy, pleeeese." Carolyn looked at Mommy imploringly, but Mommy continued to dust.

"Carolyn, your Mommy is busy. Now sit back down in front of me so I can finish."

Carolyn obeyed grudgingly. This was the third morning of Sheila's torturous tugging and Carolyn was not going to endure another one tomorrow. She sat on the carpet with her bottom lip stuck out, tears in her eyes, an angry scowl on her face and her arms crossed.

Sheila struck another snarl and Carolyn said, "Yeooow!" She grabbed her hair and jumped to her feet. "No more," she said. "Mommy, please, no more."

"But you still have snarls in your hair."

"Mommy," Carolyn pleaded. Mommy looked over at her.

"I think that's enough for today," she told Sheila diplomatically.

"Well, her hair's going to be a lot worse tomorrow if I don't get the snarls out today."

There isn't going to be a tomorrow at your hands if I can help it, Carolyn thought crossly. She rubbed her head as she left the room and Cousin Sheila behind.

Later that day Mommy suggested that Sheila take Douglas and Carolyn strawberry picking. She reached into a cupboard and brought out three plastic containers of various sizes. Each had a handle to make carrying them easier. Sheila took the largest one.

"If you fill them up I'll bake a pie. Daddy brought me in some rhubarb so I can make a strawberry-rhubarb pie for dessert."

"But, Mommy," Carolyn said as she looked at the smallest container, "it's too big to fill up."

"Alright, then, see how many you can pick compared to how many Doug and Sheila pick."

That challenge pleased Carolyn. She was going to show Mommy what a good worker she was. Better than fat old Sheila.

Sheila took her time climbing the hill. The meadow was green, the woods beyond were in full leaf. A cow mooed for her calf and it answered back. Somewhere, far away, was the steady hum of the tractor.

The tiny, red berries grew on the curve of the hill. Carolyn didn't like strawberries so she didn't eat any of the sweet, ripe fruit, but Doug did until Sheila made him stop. Carolyn picked the berries as fast as she could, but even so Dougie and Sheila had more in their pails than she had in hers.

But Carolyn was very proud of her accomplishment. She couldn't wait to show Mommy. She turned to start back, but Sheila made her wait.

"Let's go out into the road to walk down the hill. It's easier than walking down the grassy slope."

So instead of going the usual way home Sheila led them across the meadow. When they arrived at the edge there was a deep ditch they had to jump in order to reach the road.

Bossy Sheila wanted them to dump their berries in with hers.

"You can't jump over to the other side without spilling your berries. My pail is deeper than yours, so give me your strawberries and I'll pour them into my pail, then you can jump over."

"No," Carolyn said when Sheila reached for her pail.

"Carolyn, you can't jump over this ditch without

spilling your berries. Give it to me and I'll empty it into mine."

"No," Carolyn said. She wasn't going to go home without any berries in her pail to show Mommy.

Why did Sheila always have to do everything the hard way, anyway. They should have walked down the meadow to where the opening was that Daddy used to drive the tractor through. Then they wouldn't have encountered this ditch.

Carolyn said as much to Sheila. "I'm going back down the meadow."

"I don't think that's a very good idea, Carolyn."

"I don't care what you think. I'm going anyway."

"I'll tell your mother you didn't mind me. Dougie give me your berries."

Dougie handed his berries over to Sheila. She dumped them into her pail. Then he jumped over the ditch, landing safely in the road on the other side.

"Now, see what a good boy your brother is? Give me your pail." Sheila grabbed for it, but Carolyn quickly whisked it away.

"Come on, Carolyn, give her your pail so we can go home," Doug pleaded.

"No!"

"Okay, then, but I warn you, you'll spill all your berries," said dumb, old Sheila. Carolyn stuck her tongue out at her behind her back.

Sheila, for all her bulk, jumped over the ditch without much trouble. But Carolyn knew from experience that her jump would fall short because her legs weren't long enough. What she couldn't understand, though, was why Sheila wasn't willing to hold her pail for her while she jumped. Why was it so important for Sheila to dump Carolyn's berries into her own pail.

But it was. And it was equally important to Carolyn

to show Mommy how many berries she had picked all on her own.

Carolyn backed up. She braced one leg in back of the other one like she had seen her brother do. Then she ran, flew through the air and landed. Dougie grabbed her before she fell backwards into the ditch. She still had her pail in her hand. She felt triumphant!

"See, I told you. You should have listened to me. Most of your berries are down there now."

Carolyn looked. Her pail was nearly empty. The berries had flown out and landed in the dirt road and the ditch. Disappointed and angry Carolyn marched stiff legged down the hill toward home.

Inside the kitchen Mommy was rolling out pie dough when the disgruntled trio arrived at her door. Sheila told Mommy all about how Carolyn acted selfishly and very stubbornly.

"We would have a lot more berries now if Carolyn had allowed me to dump them all together into my pail. She wouldn't have lost them that way."

Carolyn felt hot, angry tears burning her eyes.

"That's not true. I picked a lot and I wanted to show you. See, they were all the way up to here in the pail." Carolyn placed her finger to the spot where she believed the lost berries had been.

Sheila declared herself hot and tired. "I'm going upstairs to my room so I can rest before supper."

Dougie left too. Carolyn went with Mommy into the pantry to watch her pick over and wash the berries.

"Mommy, Sheila wasn't being fair. She could have held my pail while I jumped. I wanted to show you how many I picked by myself."

"I know, baby, I know," Mommy said soothingly. Carolyn had an angry bright red mark on each cheek.

"Sheila is a guest in our home. It's our responsibility to be nice to her even when we don't feel like it."

Carolyn pouted. She never felt like being nice to Sheila. Why did she have to come here for her darn old vacation anyway? She said as much to Mommy.

"We're her family. The only family she's got since both her Mom and Dad died. She gets lonesome for us. I know it's harder for you when she's here, but it's only going to be for a little while longer. Try to be nice."

"I can't be nice to her. She pulls my hair. I want you to brush my hair in the morning instead of her, but she wants to do it."

"It's because she wants a little girl and a family to love and take care of. She's at that age when most girls get married. Don't you feel just a little bit sorry for her that she can't get a boyfriend?"

"I guess so." Carolyn did feel just a little bit guilty. "But don't you feel sorry for me that I have to have her brush my hair?"

Mommy laughed. She wiped her wet, stained fingers on a towel. Then she tilted Carolyn's face up toward hers by placing her hand under her small daughter's chin. She looked her straight in the eye.

"If I promise that tomorrow and every day after while she's here I brush your hair and braid it for you will you promise to be nice to her?"

Carolyn smiled too. She shook her head yes and then gave Mommy a hug.

The next morning Sheila came out of the bathroom with the hairbrush in her hand. Carolyn had a moment of sheer panic before Mommy laid her dust cloth down. She put out her hand for the brush.

"I promised Carolyn that I would brush her hair out for her this morning," she said in a gentle, no nonsense voice.

Sheila slapped the brush onto the palm of Mommy's outstretched hand.

Satisfied, Carolyn sat on the floor at Mommy's feet. Her head was still tender from yesterday's treatment of it so Mommy was extra careful.

Sheila picked up the dusting where Mommy left off, but not enthusiastically.

"You're much better at this than I am, Aunt Pearl. Why don't you take over here and I'll brush Carolyn's hair for you?"

Carolyn's head jerked around. She stared at Sheila.

Then Carolyn felt Mommy's hand on her shoulder. "That's alright, Sheila. I know you want to help, but I'm used to doing both of these tasks every morning so why don't you just sit down and relax. I'll finish Carolyn's hair first, then I'll dust."

Cousin Sheila dropped the dust cloth like it was a hot brick. "Sure, Aunt Pearl, whatever you say." She sat down across from Mommy and began to talk. With a sigh of relief Carolyn settled back against the couch. Mommy's fingers were lovingly tender on her hair.

> *You are ready with a plentiful supply of love and kindness. Now answer my prayer and rescue me as you promised.* Psalms 69:13b

Chapter 18

❦

Daddy

"We won't have too many more warm, sunny days like this one," Daddy said.

It was fall, the first crisp days of autumn. Douglas had already left for school, but Carolyn was still too little to go. By the time she woke up in the morning the big yellow school bus had already transported her brother into another world.

Carolyn ate a hot bowl of Maltex for breakfast with Daddy, with real, fresh cream skimmed from the top of the milk tank.

Every morning Daddy rose early and left the house to go down to the barn where he milked, fed, and watered the cows. He did all this before he ate his breakfast. That's why Carolyn could eat with him.

After breakfast he usually went out to work in the fields. Today he told Mommy that he planned to spread some more fertilizer while there was still good weather.

He wanted to get the manure pile down before the first snows came.

Daddy wore glasses, but Carolyn could still see his eyes. Sometimes they were brown and other times they were hazel. They changed with the weather.

Today they were brown. He finished his cereal and then he stood up. "I want to get started right away on that manure pile before it freezes."

"Can I come with you, Daddy?" Carolyn asked hopefully.

When he stood up he looked tall. His dimples showed when he smiled at her.

"Yes, you can go with me, but you better hurry and finish your breakfast."

Daddy kissed Mommy and off he went to the horse barn where the tractor was kept. Soon thereafter Carolyn heard the tractor engine start up. She jumped down from the breakfast table and hurried for her coat. But before she reached it Mommy stopped her to wipe her hands and face with a damp cloth and then dry them on a clean towel so that they wouldn't get chapped from the cool air. Then she made sure that Carolyn's coat was properly buttoned and her hat tied on tight. Her two black braids hung down on either side of her face below her collar so Mommy gently pulled them out and placed them on top of the coat.

Carolyn was anxious. She didn't want Daddy to leave without her. He had told her to hurry, but it seemed to Carolyn that Mommy was taking too long a time to finish dressing her warmly for the chill of the day. She stretched her neck to see out the window, but from that angle she couldn't see the horse barn at all.

Mommy, detecting her concern, reassured her that Daddy wouldn't leave without her.

Even so, Carolyn was worried. She could hear the

tractor, but she couldn't see it, and it bothered her to know that it was running even though the sound stayed steady. It wasn't moving yet. She reasoned that it meant he hadn't driven away yet. Still, she was very impatient for Mommy to finish.

Mommy was always very careful about Carolyn's health and safety. So while Carolyn wiggled and squirmed Mommy patiently pushed her mittens onto her little hands and then tied her shoe laces in a double knot so they would stay tied and Carolyn wouldn't be apt to trip on them and fall.

When she was finished she placed her two hands on each of Carolyn's shoulders. She bent over so she could be at eye level. Then she reminded her precious daughter of the dangers of walking behind the tractor if Daddy was backing it out of the barn.

"Wait on the side of the road until Daddy sees you so that way he won't run over you by accident. Understand?"

Carolyn understood perfectly, and what's more, she always remembered because Mommy reminded her so often. Restless to be off she quickly nodded her head. Mommy kissed her soft cheek and opened the door. Carolyn scampered through it, down the cement steps and across the lawn. She remembered to look both ways before crossing the dirt road, although there was hardly any traffic that went past, and then she was on the other side and running toward the horse barn.

She could still hear the tractor engine, but Daddy hadn't moved it yet. She stood on the side of the road and carefully peeked around the corner until she could see Daddy. He was doing something to the engine at the front of the tractor so she decided that it was safe to approach the great, green machine.

She needed help to get onto the seat, so Daddy

picked her up and swung her easily onto it. She landed with a thud on the inflexible, black cushioned seat. She moved way over to the right where Daddy had placed a board as a make-shift seat for her to sit on while he drove the tractor.

He was still tinkering with the engine. She watched while he checked the oil, added more to it, checked the pistons, the battery, and other things she didn't know about. It seemed to take forever until he was ready to go.

Then he was on the seat next to her and they were off to the barnyard to hook up the manure spreader. Daddy backed the tractor against the hitch very slowly and then, bump, it hit just right against the tractor hitch. He got off the tractor, hooked the spreader to the tractor hitch, then climbed back on. They drove down the road until he reached the flat section where he could drive the tractor into the meadow that was behind the house. Once again Daddy dismounted from the tractor, but this time he went to the back of the spreader and turned a lever so that the manure would spray out the back evenly.

Carolyn moved way over so Daddy would have room to swing his leg up over the seat and then he was sitting down and they were off.

They didn't say a word to each other because the noise from the engine was so great. She knew she couldn't distract him by touching him or the steering wheel or else they might have an accident. She had heard the story of a man who was crushed to death when his tractor tipped over so she sat very still, hardly daring to move. It was a hilly meadow and when the tractor tipped sideways on the hillside she was afraid. She anxiously searched Daddy's face and found it to be calm as usual, so she knew they were in no danger of tipping completely over and rolling the tractor.

She was nervous, though, until they were safely on level ground. Soon the manure spreader was empty and they were back to the barn to fill it up again. She waited on the seat for him to finish. It didn't take him very long even though the spreader held a lot because he was very strong.

Daddy didn't talk while he worked. But that was okay. It was enough that she was near him on the seat and they were off to finish fertilizing the meadow behind the house in the bright sunshine and fresh air.

> *But even so, you love me! You will keep on guiding me all my life with your wisdom and counsel. I desire no one on earth as much as you! He is the strength of my heart; he is mine forever!* Psalms 73:23-26

Chapter 19

The Sugar Sand

Carolyn loved going out to the gravel pit to play. She brought with her a red plastic pail, a spoon and several different sizes of tins. She used them to make pretend cakes, cookies, and pies. She added stones to the mixture for raisins or nuts. Then she would make believe to serve it to her guests. Mmmm! Everyone complimented her on her culinary ability.

Mommy let her go out every day when the sun shone. She spent many happy hours playing in the sand. Then one day after Carolyn overheard Daddy say that soon the ground would freeze, she realized that the sand in the gravel pit would be frozen, too, and then soon after covered with snow.

That wasn't such a bad thing because she and Dougie used that hill to slide down during the winter months. But it saddened her to think that she wouldn't be able to cook anymore pretend meals until next summer.

Carolyn wondered what she could do. She didn't want to wait all winter before she could play in the sand. She picked up a handful of the fine stuff. She shook it, feeling the soft warmth of it. Then she let it sift through her fingers, watching intensely as it floated to the ground.

She thought and thought. Then she decided.

She began to fill the red pail with sand. She wasn't going to spend the whole winter without her pleasurable pastime.

She carried the pail into the kitchen. Mommy saw her coming and met her at the door.

"What are you doing bringing sand into the house?"

"I want to keep it in the cupboard so I can play with it this winter."

"Oh, no, you don't," Mommy said, much to Carolyn's surprise. "That sand is dirty. It's probably filled with germs. It's not coming into my house. Go dump it back where you got it from."

"But, Mommy . . ."

"No buts about it. Bring it back to the gravel pit."

"But it's going to snow soon. I heard Daddy say so."

"You'll have to wait until next spring before you can play with it again, honey. That's just the way it is. I'm sorry, but you can't bring it into the house."

Carolyn walked slowly back to the gravel pit. She understood why Mommy wouldn't let her bring the sand into the house, but she sure wished she could find some sand that didn't have germs in it.

She dumped the pail of sand back out. Her bottom lip was hanging low. Her brow was puckered as she thought about the situation.

So Mommy won't let me bring sand into the house. What can I use instead?

Mommy had told her she couldn't bring sand into the house. What was like sand? Carolyn knew! She hurried home with her pail. Mommy didn't mind if the pail was in the house as long as it was empty.

The first chance she got Carolyn pulled the pail out. She stood on her tiptoes to look into the sugar canister. It was nearly full. She took the green cup from the top of the canister and began to place the sugar into her pail.

The first snows came, but Carolyn didn't mind because far back in one of the pantry cupboards was her red pail, ready to play with. She only took it out when Mommy was occupied some place else in the house or outside hanging laundry. She knew she was sneaking and she didn't feel good about it, but she didn't want Mommy to find out about it and make her throw it away, or worse still, spank her for using her sugar to play with.

In no time at all the sugar turned a light shade of brown.

One day, as Carolyn was coming down the hall from the living room, she heard Mommy talking to Daddy. She heard her name mentioned. She stopped. Motionless, breathless she listened.

"Look what I found pushed way in the back of one of my cupboards. It's Carolyn's red pail. I told her she couldn't bring sand into the house, but I've never seen sand like this before. Where do you think she found it?"

Carolyn took a quick peek around the corner. Daddy was sitting in the chrome rocking chair. He held the pail in his hands.

"This isn't sand," he said. "It's either salt or sugar." He tasted it. Then he handed the pail back to Mommy. "It's sugar," he said.

Carolyn didn't stick around to hear any more. She scooted back into the living room as soundlessly as possible to avoid detection.

"That little dickens," Mommy said fondly. "Imagine her thinking of such a thing."

Daddy laughed. "She didn't disobey you. She didn't bring sand into the house."

"What do you think I should do about it?"

"Put it back where you found it. It's no good to you now and there's no sense in throwing it out. Let her play with it."

Carolyn waited with dread for Mommy or Daddy to scold her about the sugar sand. But, when several days went by and nothing was said she became curious. She went into Mommy's cupboard. Standing there was her red pail just like she had left it.

She began to play with it again. Mommy came into the pantry. When she saw her sitting on the floor playing she smiled at her. Surprised, Carolyn smiled back. With relief Carolyn made her make-believe cakes. She no longer had to hide what she was doing.

When she was all done there was a little pile of sugar left on the floor. Mommy got out her broom and swept it up.

In a moment of anger I turned my face a little while; but with everlasting love I will have pity on you . . . Isaiah 54:8a

Chapter 20

Daddy and the Fiddle

Carolyn had been sick for a week. She was still coughing, but she didn't have a fever today.

She went over to the window. It was frosted over so she began to scrape it with her fingernail. It was something to do while she waited for Mommy to change the bedding on the couch.

She looked outside. The white snow was blinding with the sunlight on it. The mail box by the side of the road was nearly buried under the snow bank. Each time the snowplow went down the road the mailbox suffered an indirect hit. The silver box sat lopsided on the fence post.

Carolyn placed her chin in her hands, both elbows on the wide windowsill. She watched Daddy walk down the narrowly shoveled path toward the barn. He had a heavy pail in each hand. Carolyn could see the steam rising from them.

When he reached the mailbox he paused. Lowering the pails to the ground he stopped at the mailbox. He put his foot against the base to straighten it out as much as possible with the ground frozen and the mounds of snow encumbering his effort. He raised the red flag at its side, the signal for the mailman to stop. He opened the front of it to leave the letter Mommy had written to Mim for the mailman to pick up.

During the winter when it was harder to travel because of the ice and snow Mommy kept in touch with her mother through the mail. The cost was only a nickel a stamp, which was much less than a toll call to Burlington.

Daddy picked up the two pails of hot water and carried them into the barn. She had overheard Daddy tell Mommy that the pipes in the barn were frozen so he had to walk down to the brook and break the ice to water the cows that morning. He used an axe to chop the ice in the brook apart. It was thick and hard to chop through. He could only make a small opening which began to freeze over again almost immediately.

Then he had to let the cows out of the barn a few at a time. They didn't like walking through the snow to reach the brook so Daddy had to direct them. It was cold work especially with the wind chill factor at 20° below zero.

He was going back down to the barn with the buckets of boiling water to pour down the sink in an effort to free the frozen pipes and keep them from bursting.

The ones that were visible in the milkhouse were well wrapped with rags to keep them from freezing. But the ones that were underground were the ones that he was worried about.

After Mommy helped Carolyn lay down, she went out to the kitchen for the molasses and ginger that Daddy had made up. Mommy stirred it around and around in the cup. Then she took out a big spoonful of the awful stuff.

"Open wide," she told Carolyn.

It tasted like molasses with a bite to it. Daddy made it every time someone had a cold. It was supposed to build up their blood. Carolyn tried to swallow it, but she had to chew it a little bit first. When she was finally successful, she shivered from the effort.

"Do you think Daddy will play his fiddle for us tonight?" Carolyn asked hopefully. The taste of molasses still lingered in her mouth.

"I don't know, honey. This bad spot of weather we've been having has made him a lot of extra work. He might be too tired after supper."

Carolyn sighed deeply. She so loved to hear Daddy play the fiddle.

As the day wore on Carolyn asked Mommy time and again if Daddy was going to play his fiddle. If he wasn't too tired, she said.

"Will you ask him, Mommy?"

Mommy said she would ask him. When Dougie came in from the school bus Carolyn solicited his help in persuading Daddy, too.

Tonight was the first time that Carolyn felt well enough to sit at the table to eat with the rest of the family. She was famished. Mommy made hash from left-over roast beef, diced potatoes and onions. She put them all together in an iron skillet, covered them with water, and let them boil until they were soft and the water was gone. She served the hash with toast and butter. It was delicious.

After supper, Daddy sat tiredly in the rocking chair. Mommy felt sorry for him, but she had promised Carolyn.

"The children want to know if you'll play a song on the fiddle for them tonight."

He took off one shoe, then the other. He dropped them next to the rocking chair. He reached down to pull his brown slippers from under the stand. "No, I'm too tired," he said.

"Oh, please, Daddy, please," Douglas and Carolyn pleaded together.

Daddy pushed his feet into the slippers. The wood floor was cold.

"Not tonight."

Carolyn's face fell. She was so disappointed she wanted to cry.

Daddy noticed. He gave in. "Alright," he said as he smiled at her.

Mommy went into her bedroom closet where Daddy's fiddle was kept. It was in a black case with soft blue lining on the inside.

Daddy took it carefully out of the box, along with the bow. He fitted it on his shoulder, resting his chin against the edge.

Daddy wasn't a violin player. He fiddled. His was toe tapping, hand clapping, dancing music. When Daddy played he put his whole body into it. His foot bounced up and down as it kept time with the music. The bow moved quickly against the strings.

Carolyn sat on the braided carpet that covered the middle of the kitchen floor, hugging her knees to her chest. She had on an undershirt, a long flannel nightgown, heavy socks that went to her knees, warm slippers, and a chenille bathrobe. She watched raptly as Daddy sawed back and forth on his violin.

Daddy played several different pieces. When he put the violin down Carolyn and Dougie yelled, "More, more," but Daddy shook his head.

"I don't know any more. Pepe does. He can play better than I can. He use to play at all the barn dances. He learned to play by ear, but he couldn't pass it on. I only know the ones I already played."

Carolyn wasn't satisfied yet. "Play them again," she begged.

"I'm tired of playing the same tunes over and over again. How about if I play the harmonica instead?"

Doug and Carolyn cheered while Mommy went into the pantry for it. On the top shelf of her dish cupboard was the silver harmonica. She brought it to Daddy. He raised it to his lips.

When he played it his cheeks puffed in and out, while his foot kept time to the music. He played and played until he couldn't play anymore.

"It takes a lot of wind," he said, all out of breath. Then he tapped the harmonica, hole side down, against his hand before he gave it to Mommy to put it away.

Carolyn and Dougie wanted to hear more. They begged, but Daddy was too winded.

When Mommy came back from the pantry she handed him what looked to Carolyn like a piece of wire. "This doesn't take much wind," she said slyly.

Daddy took it with a smile. He raised it to his mouth.

The sound that came from it was a twang. It was a song, but it wasn't a tune like the other instruments played. It went boing, boing, boing, boing, boing.

"What is it?" Carolyn wanted to know.

"It's a Jew's harp."

Daddy played another tune on it before he handed it back to Mommy. "That's all for tonight," he told the children. "It's past your bedtime."

"My goodness, I didn't realize how late it was," Mommy said.

Carolyn jumped to her feet and spun around in a circle. She felt as light as a feather caught in a wind storm.

> *Silver and gold have I none; but such as I have give I thee.* Acts 3:6

Chapter 21

Red In the Snow

It was Saturday. The smell of spring was in the air even though there was still plenty of snow left on the ground.

It was good packing snow. Carolyn and Douglas were outside in their snowsuits rolling large balls to make a snowman. It was hard work to push against the giant snowball and make it move an inch or two. Carolyn glanced over at Dougie. His was bigger and he didn't seem to be having the trouble moving it like she was with hers.

Mommy came out on the front porch steps. She had on her customary house dress. She wore only dresses, Carolyn had never seen her in pants.

Daddy had rigged a clothesline for her off the porch. It was a thick piece of rope, looped around a pulley on each end. One was attached to the house, the other to a maple tree across the front yard. That way the line was up above anyone walking, but it was easily accessible to Mommy when she stood on the porch steps.

She placed her basket of clean clothes on the floor of the porch and left the door open. There it was closer for her to pick out a piece of laundry from the pile and the bottom of the basket stayed out of the snow.

She had more lines around the side of the house next to the old chicken coop that were already filled, so Carolyn knew that Mommy's washing was almost done.

Mommy was very fussy about how her wash looked out on the line. She always placed her clothes in order before she came out to hang them. Her towels were all together by style and color, then her face cloths, her dishtowels and dishcloths, any of Daddy's shirts came before his jeans or overalls. Doug's clothes were hung together before Carolyn's.

"Whew," Carolyn said as she leaned back against her half of the snowman. She had tried with all her might, but she couldn't push it any further.

Dougie was finished with the bottom half so he came over to help her. They pushed it toward his so that the snowman would have a middle. Then Carolyn decided Dougie could lift it onto the base by himself. Besides, she was too tired to help any more.

That's when she saw the red on the snow.

Her eyes quickly moved to the source of the blood. Mommy!

"Mommy, Mommy, you're bleeding," Carolyn screamed.

Mommy just smiled her serene smile. "I know I am, but it's alright."

But Dougie and Carolyn didn't think so. The snowman partly finished and forgotten they pleaded with Mommy to come in to the house with them.

"When I finish hanging this last batch of laundry, then I will."

While Dougie ran to the barn for Daddy, Carolyn hovered close to Mommy, handing her each piece of wet clothes and two clothespins. Finally, the basket was empty. Carolyn brought it into the house. Mommy looked pale and tired. Carolyn was scared.

"What is it. Why are you bleeding? Is your leg cut?"

Carolyn bent over to look at Mommy's legs, but she didn't see any place where the blood was coming from.

Wearily, Mommy sat down on a chair. She still had her coat on even though the kitchen was very warm.

Daddy came into the house with Dougie. He looked angry.

"I thought I told you to leave the washing, that I would finish it for you when I was done with my barn chores."

So Daddy had known.

"I don't want you to do my work for me. You have enough of your own."

"You've helped me often enough in the barn when I've needed it."

"I know, but that's different."

"How, how is it different."

"The farm is our living. You needed the help."

"You are my wife." Daddy emphasized the words. "Nothing is more important to me than you are."

Mommy's eyes filled up with tears.

Gentler than before Daddy asked if Mommy wanted him to call the doctor.

"No. Don't bother. I know what he's going to tell me. Go to bed, put my feet up higher than my head. But I can't go to bed. I have two small children and a house to take care of."

"Go to bed, if you need to. I'll take care of them and the house."

"No, Ray, you can't. It's too much with everything else you have to do. I'm not going to go to bed."

When she saw that he was going to insist she continued. "The worse is over, I know it is. On the first good day we have, when the roads are all clear and we know we can get back home, we'll go to Burlington to see the gynecologist. Meanwhile, I'll take it easy. I promise."

Daddy knew that was the best compromise he was going to get. Wordlessly he went over to Mommy's wringer washing machine and began to empty the water out of it.

Over his shoulder he said, "I'll bring in the clothes later. I don't want you to do it."

"If I think I can manage it I'm going to and if not then I'll let you. Carolyn can help me."

"Then let her do most of it. Don't let Mommy reach over her head, Carolyn. You do that for her." Then in French he added, "Understand?"

Carolyn nodded solemnly.

"Ray, she's just a little girl."

Daddy looked Carolyn over. "She's big enough," he said.

Dougie dragged a chair over so Mommy could rest

her feet on it. Carolyn stood real close to Mommy as if to protect her. Mommy had never been sick before.

When Daddy was finished he placed the washing machine back over in the corner where it went when it wasn't being used. He made lunch and served it. Then he did the dishes.

Carolyn had never seen Daddy do these things before. She knew that Mommy must be real sick.

When Daddy and Dougie went back down to the barn Carolyn asked Mommy what was wrong.

"The doctor thinks I lost a baby," Mommy told her. "I don't know if it's true or not. It doesn't feel the same as the other times that I had a miscarriage."

Carolyn was more puzzled than ever. She asked Mommy what she meant.

"Before you were born, or even before Douglas, I had another baby. His name was Roger. He was born prematurely. That means too early. He weighed less than 2 pounds, but he had a full head of curly, black hair. He had big hands like your Pepe. He only lived 15 hours." She had tears in her eyes again.

"Did you get to hold him?"

"No, I didn't even get to see him."

"Then how do you know what he looked like?"

"Daddy told me. And before him I lost a little girl. She was our first Carolyn, but she was born dead so we couldn't name her. I lost two other babies before I had Doug. We were married for thirteen years. We thought we'd never have any children, but then we moved here. The depression was over. Daddy had a steady job again. We had our own home. I met Doctor Fleming.

"He's a wonderful doctor. He knew about the four miscarriages, so when I got pregnant for Doug he had me take 32 pills a day so that I wouldn't miscarry. In order to have you I had to take the same amount. But this time I didn't know I was pregnant until it was too late."

Mommy started to cry. Carolyn wrapped her arms tightly around Mommy's neck while she sobbed deep racking sobs.

She hugged Carolyn to her. "Daddy and I prayed for years to have children. Thank God that he gave me you. What would I do without you or Doug? I would be empty, lost without you."

Carolyn understood. That's how she felt about Mommy and Daddy.

Later, Carolyn buttoned her coat, pulled on her hat and mittens. Then she dragged a kitchen chair out onto the porch step and climbed up on it. Reaching way above her head she tugged at the first clothespin. It was partially frozen to the line. When it came off she pulled the line closer in order to reach the next clothespin. She took the towel down and handed it to Mommy. It was stiff, but Mommy folded it and placed it in the bottom of the basket. It would thaw out when they brought it into the kitchen to hang from the wooden clothes rack Mommy had already placed next to the cook stove.

The snowman stood dejectedly where they had left him. His middle was on crooked and his head wasn't made yet. He was only partly formed, but he would be around tomorrow and the next day. They could finish him then.

You made all the delicate, inner parts of my body, and knit them together in my mother's womb. Thank you for making me so wonderfully complex! It is amazing to think about. Your workmanship is marvelous—and

how well I know it. You were there while I was being formed in utter seclusion! You saw me before I was born and scheduled each day of my life before I began to breathe. Every day was recorded in your Book!
Psalms 139:13-16

Chapter 22

❦

Three O'Clock Milking

At three o'clock every afternoon Daddy started calling the cows home.

"Ca'boys," he would yell. Sometimes Mommy and Carolyn would join Daddy. It was fun to yell for them to come home.

"Ca'boys," Mommy yelled. Carolyn echoed it. The cows came out of the woods and started down the lane toward the barn. They mooed in response. You can stop calling us, we're coming, they seemed to say. Dougie was behind them, driving them home.

Daddy waited at the double doors for the cows to come in. They started up the ramp, some of them crowded together, others patiently waited for their turn. Sometimes two would come into the barn together, but each went to her own stanchion. They were all anxious to be milked, for their bags were full and uncomfortable.

When the cows stuck their heads into the stanchions someone would push it shut, the board at the top would fall into place and the cow would be locked in. Carolyn had to stand on her tiptoes to accomplish this feat, but she didn't mind. It was fun to help with the milking. They all did their part.

Once the cows were in the barn Daddy began the arduous task of washing the bags with a clean cloth soaked in a pail of warm sudsy water in order that no bacteria would contaminate the milk. Then he would set one of the milking machines next to the clean cow. Swinging the three-legged milk stool near the animal, he would sit down on it. Then, with his left hand he balanced the four suction cups from the milking machine. He lifted one at a time.

Thwoup! went the first one as it grabbed onto the cows udder. Thwoup, thwoup, thwoup! Then he turned a lever and the machine began milking the cow while she calmly stood and chewed her cud.

With two milking machines, one on each side of the barn, Daddy worked his way from cow to cow. When one of the cans was full he unscrewed the top of it. Inside lay the warm, frothy milk. He picked up the heavy milk can and balanced it on his knee before he poured the milk into one of the smaller pails. Then either he, Mommy or Doug would bring it into the milkroom to pour it into the big milk tank.

When the cow's bag was empty the suction cups

came off easily. Then Daddy stripped each one by hand to get out the last of the milk. If he didn't, the cow would get mastitis, which would cause contamination in the milk. When that happened to a farmer the milk plant wouldn't buy the milk. If they didn't buy the milk the farmer wouldn't get paid until the mastitis was cleared up. A vet would come to treat the cow and the state would close the farmer down until one of the state inspectors could come back to declare the milk safe again. It was one of the hazards of running a dairy farm, a hazard Daddy was very careful to avoid.

Daddy kept his cows and barn clean. Along with washing the cows he also clipped the hair off their backsides with a shaver whenever they needed it. And in the spring a man came to whitewash the barn. He used a big sprayer to shoot the mixture of lime and water over all the walls, ceiling, stanchions, cement floor and double doors. It cleansed the barn from bacteria and other germs while it whitened the surface.

The man wore clothing that made him look like an astronaut. No one was allowed inside while he was whitewashing. Afterwards the barn was transformed from dingy to gleaming white. But the disinfectant burned Carolyn's nose and made her head ache until Daddy opened the windows to let some fresh air in.

Every day of the year, even Sundays and holidays Daddy milked the cows at three o'clock. Sometimes, on a Sunday after church, they would visit one of Mommy's relatives. Her brother, Uncle Reggie, lived in Winóoski. He owned an old house that he had converted into an upstairs apartment. He and his wife and their three sons lived on the first floor. A nice, quiet, newlywed couple occupied the upstairs.

There was a wrap-around porch on the house.

Carolyn enjoyed running along it with her cousins, until Aunt Marcella made them stop.

Aunt Marcella was a good cook, but not as good as Mommy. Still, Carolyn was full from the roast beef, new potatoes baked in their skins, sweet rolls, and the Apple Pie àla mode that Aunt Marcella had served for dinner.

Soon, more company arrived until the house was filled to over flowing. Daddy and the rest of the men played horseshoes in the backyard, while the women chatted in the living room about children, chores, money and husbands.

Dougie was in the front bedroom with Mike, who was Aunt Marcella's oldest son. He and Doug were the same age.

It seemed like there was activity in every room. The time passed very quickly.

When 2 o'clock arrived Daddy began to fidget. He stuck his hand in the pocket of his suit pants and began to jingle the loose change there. Sooner or later one of the men would notice that Daddy wasn't paying attention to the game at hand.

"The cows calling, Ray?"

"He can hear them all the way from Richmond. Time to get home for the three o'clock milking."

It was an old joke among Mommy's relatives. They knew that whenever Daddy was away from the farm, no matter where they were or how much fun they were having, he would start jingling his change when it was time to go home to milk the cows.

For all their teasing Mommy's brothers admired Daddy. "It must be getting close to milking time. He's starting to get nervous," they said. Then everyone would laugh, even Daddy. He would leave the men to find Mommy.

"Pearl," he said from the door of the living room.

"I'm coming," she answered. She knew, too, that it was time to milk the cows. She called to Doug and Carolyn.

During the winter months Sunday's were spent at home. On good days, when it didn't snow, the relatives would brave the country hills for a visit.

They would start to arrive soon after church. First Mommy's brother, Uncle Allie and his wife Aunt Dorrie would come with their four children. Then, one of Mommy's other brothers or her sisters or sometimes several of them would stop by. The dinner table was full of food and laughter and the afternoon passed pleasantly.

By a few minutes before 3 o'clock Daddy would change his clothes and head down for the barn. Sometimes one of the relatives would accompany him, but most of the time he went alone. He enjoyed the solitude of the barn after the raucous festivity in the house. Here, among his animals, he was content.

> *To enjoy your work and to accept your lot in life—that is indeed a gift from God. The person who does that will not need to look back with sorrow on his past, for God gives him joy.*
> Ecclesiastes 5:20

Chapter 23

School Days

"Oh, my God, what happened to you?"

Dougie had gotten off the school bus. He had blood on his shirt and coat. When he came into the house he was crying. Between sobs Douglas told the story.

"I was skating on the ice in back of the school building when someone came up behind me and pushed me real hard. I fell on the ice and hit my nose. It started to bleed."

"Who pushed you, Doug?"

But Dougie wouldn't tell on his friend.

"Why didn't you call us. We would have come after you."

"When the bell rang I told my teacher that I wanted to call you because my nose hurt so bad, but she wouldn't let me. She made me sit down at my desk."

"When did this happen?"

"This morning before school started."

Mommy was outraged. She had Dougie lay down

on the couch. His nose was bent over to one side. He had a black eye. She placed a cold compress over his nose and eyes.

While he lay there she went down to the barn. A few minutes later she returned. Then she called the doctor.

She told him what had happened on the playground and asked him if he could wait until Daddy was done with the chores. It might be after 5 o'clock, which was past his office hours, but the doctor said he would wait for as long as was necessary. Mommy thanked him and hung up the phone.

While she waited for Daddy to finish his chores she called the teacher at home.

"Why didn't you call when Doug got hurt?" she asked.

"I didn't think he was hurt that badly. It was only a bruise."

"Only a bruise! He has a broken nose."

"How do you know. Has he seen a doctor?"

"No, but he's going to just as soon as we can get him there. Anyone can tell his nose is broken. It's bent over to one side. Even if it isn't broken he was still hurt. You had no right to keep it from us. We are his parents and it is for us to decide if he needs medical attention or not."

The teacher apologized. She knew Mommy was right.

Daddy finished his chores as quickly as possible. While he washed up Mommy got Carolyn and Dougie ready.

It was just after 5 o'clock when they reached the doctors office. He was waiting for them. The doctor brought them into the last examining room on the right.

Mommy wouldn't let Carolyn come into the room. "Wait out here for us," she said.

Carolyn waited outside the door. She leaned against the wall. When Dougie began to cry Carolyn could bear it no longer. She walked down the long hall until she reached the end. A window over the door revealed that the sun was setting. She could still hear Douglas wailing.

Nervously she walked back down the hall toward the sound of Doug's crying. The door was slightly ajar. Carolyn tried to see into the room, but the door blocked her view. She heard Dougie pleading with Mommy and Daddy. She heard the doctors calm voice. She heard Daddy reassure Doug.

Then she heard Doug scream.

She began pacing the floor in front of the door, wishing with all her might that she could go in to see for herself what was happening.

After what seemed an eternity the door opened.

Dougie was as limp as a rag doll. His brown eyes were bugged out, his face a deathly white. His eyelids were red and puffy. On his nose was a steel bridge with a white bandage over it to keep it in place.

The doctor gave Mommy a small packet. "This is to help him sleep through the night," he said. "Put it in a glass of warm milk and stir it until it's all dissolved." Mommy and Daddy thanked the doctor. Then Mommy asked what they owed him.

"Not a thing," he said.

"But, Doctor," Mommy began.

"My office closed at 5 o'clock. I don't receive patients after that, only friends."

Daddy shook Dr. Fleming's hand.

The next day there was an article in the Burlington

paper. It said that Little Raymond Dupont had fallen on the playground at school and broken his nose.

It was the understatement of the year.

You have collected all my tears and preserved them in your bottle! You have recorded every one in your book. Psalm 56:8b

Chapter 24

The Yellow Jackets

"Want to see something?" Dougie asked Carolyn.

"What is it?"

"C'mon. I'll show you."

It was after supper, but still light out. They went around the side of the house toward the old chicken coop.

It hadn't held chickens for years. Daddy had converted it to an open tool shed. Daddy kept the circular saw there. It was easier to bring it from the chicken coop to the woodshed where he would cut the larger pieces of firewood down to manageable sizes that would fit in the wood stove. It had a thin flat blade with a line of sharp teeth around its edge. It ran with a belt and a motor. Daddy would guide the wood down the shaft that led to the saw. He would push it through very carefully so the saw wouldn't cut his hand off. The saw was so sharp it would cut a large piece of hard wood like butter.

The shed also had Daddy's old scythe in it. He didn't use it for anything except to mow down the tall grass that grew between the lawn and the meadow behind the house. But it was still very sharp.

Carolyn wasn't allowed inside the chicken coop because of the dangerous equipment, but Dougie could go inside since he was older. What he wanted to show her was only a few feet inside the opened end.

"Look, up there. Do you see that cone shaped gray nest?" Douglas pointed to the rafters of the chicken coop. Carolyn searched the ceiling with her eyes.

"Look," Dougie said again. This time he was standing almost directly under it. She nodded her head. She watched with chills as the strange creatures that inhabited the nest flew in and out.

"How did you know it was here?"

"I found it," he said proudly. "I came in here to look for something and I heard them buzzing. Daddy says they're yellow jackets. Their sting is worse than a bee sting."

Carolyn's eyes were wide with fright.

"Come on," Douglas said, placing a protective arm around her shoulders. "We don't have to stay around here." He led her back to the house. He got his bike out of the workshop, where Daddy kept tools like his hammers, screwdrivers, and other hand implements.

Dougie was stronger than Carolyn. He guided the bike easily down the cement steps. He swung his leg over the seat. Then he helped her to get on the bar in front of the seat and behind the handlebars. They went for a ride down the bumpy dirt road.

It was fun to feel the air blow across her face. She held onto the handlebars in the middle so that Douglas could steer. His two arms, one on each side of her, made her feel safe.

She didn't have her own bike yet. She was still too little for one. But she loved riding with Doug. He didn't always ask her, but oftentimes he would. They didn't go far, only to the curve in the road where they couldn't see the house anymore. That was Mommy's rule, in case the bike tipped over. If Carolyn got hurt, Doug wouldn't have to carry her too far. If Doug got hurt Carolyn would only have to yell for Mommy or Daddy to hear. Usually they rode back to the curve and then home again more than once.

"You know what I'm going to do when we get home?" Douglas said in her ear.

Carolyn shook her head.

"I'm going to get me a shovel and knock that hornet's nest down."

Back into the driveway they skidded. Doug took his feet off the pedals. He let them slide along the ground to slow the bike down. They coasted up to the house.

He put his bike away like he was supposed to. Carolyn waited outside for him. It seemed to take a long time, but when he came out she saw the reason why. He had found an old shovel to knock the nest down with.

They scooted around the corner of the house to the chicken coop.

Douglas looked at the nest, high in the rafters,

then he made a pass at it with his shovel. It barely reached.

"Make sure now, when I yell 'run' you do it as fast as you can all the way into the house. They're going to be mad as all get out when I knock it down so you better get back so you can have a head start."

Carolyn reluctantly moved back. She didn't want to go so far that she couldn't see the nest anymore.

"Keep going," her brother instructed her until he felt certain she would be safe.

"But I can't see anything way out here," she complained. He didn't seem to hear her so she came back a little ways. Bending way down she still couldn't see the nest. He made one pass at it and she started to run, but he yelled at her that he hadn't hit it yet.

She came back and this time she stood at the edge of the entrance so that she could see. He hit it once, twice, and the third time he knocked it down. He dropped the shovel and streaked past her. "Run!" he yelled.

Carolyn turned to run, but already the yellow jackets were all over her, stinging her. She kept running. Douglas had the kitchen door open and she was screaming.

Daddy and Mommy met her at the door. By this time she was crying because the angry yellow jackets were still stinging her and it hurt. She ran into the house and Mommy shut the door leaving the majority of the yellow jackets outside.

Daddy picked a total of five yellow jackets off Carolyn. He asked her where it hurt, she would show him, he would pick one off and squeeze it in his strong fingers until it was dead. He was completely unafraid of them.

A few were buzzing around the kitchen windows.

Daddy killed those too. When he didn't find any more, Mommy went into the pantry to make up an oatmeal solution to take the sting out of Carolyn's bites.

Dougie hadn't gotten stung at all.

"Daddy, my ankle hurts," Carolyn said.

Daddy picked her foot up. Her white socks were rolled down nice and neat. "I don't see anything," he said.

"Ow! Right here, Daddy." Carolyn pointed at her sock.

Daddy picked her foot up again and this time he placed it on his knee. Then he rolled the sock down. A yellow jacket, trapped under Carolyn's sock, escaped into the room. It had stung her many times around her ankle.

"By gosh, she's right," he said. "She did have another one trapped in her sock."

The yellow jacket began to fly around the kitchen until it landed on one of the windows. Daddy calmly followed its course. He waited until it was buzzing against the pane before he caught it. He picked it up between his fingers and squeezed it like he had the others.

"Why don't they sting you, Daddy?"

Mommy answered for him. "Because he isn't afraid of them."

"Daddy isn't afraid of anything, are you Daddy?" Carolyn sat on Daddy's lap in the rocking chair while Mommy applied the soothing oatmeal plaster on the bites.

Douglas didn't get stung and he didn't get punished either. Because he was scared when he knew his sister was hurt and he was responsible for it, Daddy said he figured he had learned his lesson and wouldn't make the same mistake again.

"No, sir," he said. "I sure won't do it again. The next nest I find I'll knock it down when I'm alone. Then, if anyone gets stung, it'll be me."

"No, the next nest you find you leave it alone. If it needs to be knocked down I will do it. It isn't a decision you're ready to make yet."

Dougie looked shame-faced, but Daddy smiled at him. Carolyn cuddled deeper into his lap and began to twirl her hair. Suddenly, she was very sleepy.

Rescue me, O God! Lord hurry to my aid!
Psalm 70:1

Chapter 25

The Rag Bag

"Mommy, where did you get this dress from?" Carolyn asked.

She had been rummaging around in the rag bag out in the wood shed. She had discovered a yellow satin evening gown in it. Her blue eyes sparkled with the exhilaration of such a find.

"Your cousin wore it to a dance last year. She can't wear it again this year so your Aunt Dorrie brought it up for the rag man."

"Can I play with it until he comes?"

Mommy smiled at her little girl, all lit up with excitement. She had the yellow satin dress on over her clothes. It dragged on the floor around her. One of the spaghetti straps had slipped off her shoulder, but to Mommy, Carolyn was every bit as pretty in it as her older cousin must have been when she wore it to the dance. Mommy nodded her head and Carolyn lifted the skirt so that she could walk without tripping. Happily she went back out into the woodshed to play.

Today she was a princess.

The next day at breakfast Carolyn asked Mommy when the rag man was coming.

"Soon," Mommy answered.

"Today?" Carolyn asked in distress.

"No, not that soon."

"Then can I play with the dress again?" Mommy smiled and nodded. Carolyn hopped down from the table. In the wood shed she carefully took the evening gown out of the rag bag.

Digging further into the rag bag she discovered a lace curtain that she put on her head like a veil so she could make believe she was a bride. The only problem was it kept slipping off her silky hair. Mommy helped her to fix it by pushing a bobby pin in at the top. It hurt Carolyn's head when Mommy pushed it in, but if it helped to make her beautiful than she was willing to accept the temporary discomfort.

Next she went to the meadow to pick some flowers since every bride needs a bouquet.

Later, she pretended she was a beautiful lady that all the men wanted to dance with. She held the dress up in one hand and held onto a tree limb while she waltzed with the handsome make-believe partner whose hand she held.

The next day she was Cinderella. She tied the curtain around her waist like an apron. The following day she was a movie star, the day after that a queen.

The next morning Mommy told her that she expected the rag man to arrive that day.

When Carolyn pulled the yellow evening dress out of the rag bag she felt sad. It was such a pretty dress. She wished she could keep it always. Slowly she entered the kitchen holding it and the curtain in her arms.

"Mommy, do you have to sell this dress to the rag man?"

"You like it, don't you." It was not a question since Mommy knew her little girl very well.

Carolyn nodded her head. Her eyes looked hopefully at Mommy.

"I'll make a deal with you. If you put the curtain back into the rag bag you can keep the dress."

"But why can't I have them both?" Sometimes Carolyn was selfish. She could have the dress, but that wasn't enough. However, Mommy had a surprise for her.

"I have something better for you to play with. I have a real veil that I wore when I made my First Communion. I want you to have it now."

"Oh, Mommy, really? Can I see it?"

It was so much more beautiful than the curtain. It was a cream color and it had a delicate floral design. The best thing about it was that it had been made especially to wear on a head rather than on a curtain rod. It hung gracefully down either side of Carolyn's face instead of slipping off like the curtain did.

Carolyn threw her arms around Mommy's neck

and kissed her on the cheek. "Thank you, Mommy, thank you."

When the rag man came the yellow dress was hanging safely in Carolyn's closet to be played with whenever she felt like pretending to be someone other than herself.

Ask, and it shall be given you . . . Matthew 7:7

Chapter 26

Cracks In the Road

Carolyn had overslept. The sun shone brightly around the edges of the drawn shade.

After several days and nights of rain ending with a bad thunder storm the night before, the sun streaming through Carolyn's bedroom window was a welcome sight.

She was sleeping in Doug's old bedroom off from Mommy and Daddy's room. Here the noise from the kitchen was distant so she didn't wake up as early as when she had been sleeping in the same room as Mommy and Daddy. Doug was now sleeping upstairs in the bedroom with the stovepipe in it. It was the only room upstairs that had heat in the winter.

She loved having her own bedroom and closet. She could come in any time during the day to play house with her dolls. Or she could take her doll house and doll furniture out of the walk-in closet and set them up on her bedroom floor. It was such a pleasure!

She pulled on the shade and sent it flying upward. She picked up the clothes that Mommy had laid out for her the night before on the antique chair. While she dressed, Carolyn watched a robin gather straw from the field outside the window to build a nest with. The red chested bird flew from the field with a piece of straw in its beak around the corner of the house where Carolyn couldn't see it. In a few minutes it was back for another piece of straw.

Carolyn skipped happily out into the kitchen, but much to her surprise Mommy wasn't there. She opened the door and went outside.

Mommy and Daddy were standing in front of the barn. As Carolyn approached Mommy held up her hand in front of her, as a traffic cop would do to stop a car.

"Don't try to cross the road, Carolyn."

As she neared the road Carolyn became frightened. Her pleasure turned into sharp dismay. There were deep ruts and cracks in it. And Mommy and Daddy were on the other side with Doug.

Mommy told her not to move because she could fall into one of the deep ruts and get hurt. The thought frightened Carolyn. She remained still, only her eyes moved, surveying the extensive damage.

Daddy went over to the side of the barn where he

got two long planks. He lowered them onto the road, one in front of the other. Mommy walked along them until she reached Carolyn.

Relieved that she was no longer alone, Carolyn clung to Mommy's hand.

"The rain washed out the road," Mommy explained. "You must promise me that you won't try to cross it until they come with more gravel and the grader to fix it."

Carolyn nodded.

Daddy followed Doug across the plank. Mommy voiced her concern.

"What are we going to do, Ray? I have to go to town today."

It was payday, the day that Daddy got paid for his milk. Daddy got a milk check every two weeks, or twice a month. Some months were longer than others so Mommy had to make the money stretch, as she called it. This was one of those times. Mommy just had to get to town. The electric bill had to be paid promptly or the company might shut off the power. They couldn't operate the farm without electricity. She also needed groceries.

"Don't worry. As soon as you're ready we'll go," Daddy said.

Mommy made Carolyn's breakfast. While she ate, Mommy went into her bedroom to change her dress. When she came back out Carolyn was done eating. Mommy had her purse on her arm and she was wearing a hat. She washed Carolyn's hands and face, placed the dirty dish that Carolyn had used on the counter near the sink and then they went back outside.

The road was a mess, but, like a miracle, the car was waiting for them in front of the barn. As Carolyn neared it she noticed that the tires were on planks.

Daddy brought two more planks out of the barn to place in front of it. Dougie was on his knees in the backseat trying to see past the steering wheel at what Daddy was doing.

Mommy asked Daddy if he thought they could make it downstreet.

"Sure," he said. "It'll be slow going until we get off our road, but the main road is paved, that won't be washed out. We'll make it."

He helped Mommy into the car before he carried Carolyn over. He put the car in gear. It moved slowly onto the next set of planks. His car door was still open. He stopped the car, put it in neutral, then he hopped out. Carolyn and Doug watched him through the back window. He pulled one plank out of the mud, then brought it around the car. He laid it down in front of the tire before repeating the same routine on the other side.

Since Mommy couldn't drive Daddy had to get in and out of the car many times. It was only $^1/_2$ mile to the main road, but it seemed to Carolyn to take forever. When they finally made it to the end of the dirt road Daddy removed the planks and placed them along the side where they were easily accessible for the return trip.

Daddy drove the rest of the way to Richmond without incident. Everywhere there was evidence of the storm, but the main road was clear of debris.

When they reached town Daddy turned down the dirt driveway that led to the creamery. It was full of potholes. The car bumped and jostled its way up to the large gray building.

The family went inside. Mommy needed to buy some of the creamery's sweet butter, but before she did she stopped at the desk to pick up the milk check.

"Did you hear about the mud slide that killed two people?" the secretary asked Mommy as she handed her the check.

"Yes, Ray heard it this morning on the radio in the barn."

Carolyn hadn't heard about it. She waited expectantly.

"Wasn't that terrible?" the secretary said.

"What an awful way to die." Mommy agreed.

"What happened, Mommy?"

"Two people were in a gravel pit that some of the local men and boys use to practice target shooting. Because of the recent rain we've had, plus that downpour last night, the hill gave way and it buried them."

Carolyn's stomach turned over. It was an awful way to die.

"Does anyone know who they were?" Mommy asked the secretary.

"Strangers. The speculation is that they found a quiet spot for a rendezvous of some kind. It's all very mysterious."

The secretary turned to the next farmer's wife waiting in line for her milk check. Mommy went over to buy some of the creamery's cheese and butter.

After the milk plant they went to the bank. Mommy deposited Daddy's pay into the checkbook. The tellers were talking about the tragic double deaths.

"A man and a woman. No car around. No one knows what they were doing there on that deserted stretch of road, in the middle of the night, in the worse storm we've had in years."

Daddy had an opinion. "Lost, probably, poor souls. Looking for shelter in the storm, not expecting the gravel pit to cave in on them. God bless them, their troubles are behind them now." The teller handed Mommy the deposit slip and they left the bank.

It was the same everywhere they went. All people talked about was the storm and the mud slide which had taken two lives.

Even though I walk through the valley of the shadow of death, I will fear no evil, for you are with me . . . Psalm 23:4a

Chapter 27

The Bunnies

Carolyn loved animals just like Daddy did. Someone gave her two bunnies. One was brown, the other white. She named them Fluffy and Muffy.

Their fur was soft and smooth. They had long ears that were pressed against their back. They didn't stick straight up in the air like the ones on her stuffed Easter bunny.

She spent every day playing with them. Daddy had made them a comfortable home under the horse barn where the stone foundation was partly gone. Once placed inside they couldn't escape because the stones on the very bottom of the foundation were still solid. It was a big enough opening for Carolyn to crawl into, though she didn't like the close feeling it gave her. The barn floor was just above her head and the place smelled dank.

Each morning she brought them fresh food and water. She placed the dish just inside the opening where she could reach them easily when they were finished eating.

She was afraid she would loose sight of them in the tall grass behind the barn, so when she wanted to play with them she would bring them to the front yard where the grass was shorter. Here it was easy to play with them. Under her watchful eye neither could hop too far away.

They were content to take turns on her lap. Their long ears wiggled and their nose twitched when Carolyn petted them.

Daddy observed her from the kitchen window. She was sitting on the sun-warmed cement step. "She's a real little mother," he said. "She won't leave them alone for a minute."

Mommy agreed, adding, "Won't she be surprised when Muffy has babies." Mommy and Daddy smiled at each other. They were delighted that Carolyn was enjoying her new pets so much.

"Well, it's happened," Daddy announced at breakfast the following week. "Muffy has had her babies."

Carolyn wanted to rush out to see them, but Mommy made her wait until she finished eating.

After breakfast Carolyn raced down the road to

the barn. Sure enough, there were five additions to the rabbit population. They were too far away from the opening and Carolyn didn't want to crawl in after them. She tried to coax them over, but only Fluffy responded. She petted him, but most of her attention was on the miniature bunnies that were cuddled around Muffy. Carolyn had to be content to watch them from a distance unless she wanted to crawl in there with them. She looked at the spider's webs hanging from the flooring. She definitely did not want to crawl in there with them.

Day after day she went down to the barn. Only Fluffy came to the opening. She would pet him while her eager eyes watched the tiny babies grow.

Two were brown like their mother, one was white, and two were brown and white. Carolyn strained her eyes to see them more clearly in the dim light of the barn cellar. She could hardly wait until she could take them in her arms.

Daddy came around the corner. He was smiling. "I thought I would find you here," he said. "Why aren't you in there with them?"

"I don't like it. There's spiders and bugs that live in there."

Daddy laughed. He knew how much she hated spiders and bugs.

"You can't see much from here," he said. Then, much to her surprise he crawled in under the barn floor. He gathered a couple of the babies up in his hand.

"Here," he said. He gave them to Carolyn. Then he went back for another one before he climbed out over the stone foundation.

Carolyn's eyes were shining as she gently stroked the quivering babies. Daddy was petting one, too. The bunnies smelled of earth and milk.

"That's enough for now," he told her after a few minutes. "Muffy is starting to worry. See how she's hopping around searching for her missing babies." He brought them back to their mother.

When he crawled back out he asked Carolyn if she was ready to go home.

"No, I want to stay here a little longer."

"Suit yourself," Daddy said. "If you change your mind I'll give you a ride back on the tractor." She heard him walk through the tall grass until he reached the front of the horse barn. She could hear him tinkering with his tractor. That's when she decided to leave the bunnies behind. She ran to catch up with Daddy before he left on the tractor.

The next morning Carolyn skipped down the road to the horse barn. She rounded the corner. The hay stubble was prickly here. She bent down to look inside, calling softly to the bunnies.

She wasn't prepared for the horror that met her eyes. Each bunny, even the babies, were torn to pieces. She ran down the road crying, "Daddy, Daddy, come quick. I think the bunnies are all dead."

Daddy came out of the cow barn. Carolyn was sobbing. He listened to her, his face grave. He told her to go to the house, that he didn't want her to come with him.

After she poured out her story Mommy gathered her onto her lap. She let Carolyn cry for as long as she needed to, all the while giving her what comfort she could.

Daddy came into the house. He quietly told her that he had buried them.

"They were killed quickly," he said. "I don't think they suffered much."

Mommy asked him what he thought had killed them.

"Looked like it was the neighbor's dog. I saw it sniffing around there the other day. I sent it away, but it must have gotten their scent. I should have realized it would come back. It killed just for the pleasure of killing. None of them were eaten at all."

Carolyn was so sad. She cried all the harder. It was the cruel injustice of it that hurt so much. She could picture the frightened, defenseless bunnies trying to protect their babies from a monstrous enemy, caught in a corner where there was no escape.

"Honey, we'll get you some more bunnies. I promise," Mommy said.

It didn't help.

A few days went past before Carolyn could bear to go back down to the horse barn. She stood at the corner for a few minutes, steeling herself for what was ahead.

When at last she squatted down to peer into the dim interior beyond the stone foundation, for one traumatic moment she saw the dead bunnies, the blood, the scuffled dirt. She looked closer at the dirt floor. There was nothing there at all. It was empty. Like her heart.

She left, knowing that she didn't want any more bunnies. She would tell Mommy her decision. She was safe with the stuffed Easter bunny. At least he would never die.

> *Come, Lord, and show me your mercy, for I am helpless, overwhelmed, in deep distress; my problems go from bad to worse. See my sorrows; feel my pain . . .* Psalms 25:16-18a

Chapter 28

Mommy and the Red Umbrella

"It's going to be a nice day if it don't rain," Daddy said as he came into the kitchen for breakfast. He was grinning from ear to ear. It was pouring out.

"How's the barnyard?" Mommy asked as he ate. She had made fresh doughnuts yesterday and he was dunking one in his coffee.

"It's pretty muddy, but the cows can get to the brook. I let them go to the north pasture today, up toward Dr. Devereaux's farm. After they graze a little they'll bunch up under that stand of trees by the stone fence that separates his land from ours. If it lets up they'll come home by themselves. If it doesn't they'll be close by so one of us can walk up the hill and bring them back home. Too bad Betty isn't here. She was great on days like this."

All day it rained. In the afternoon there was a thunderstorm. Mommy unplugged the television and put the picture postcard of St. Anne in the window to keep the lightening from hitting the house.

Daddy took a nap in one of the living room chairs. Mommy covered him up with a light blanket and let him sleep.

When it was time to bring the cows home Mommy told Daddy that she would help him.

"It's too wet outside to send Doug. His boots aren't waterproof either. Take the kids down to the barn with you and I'll go get the cows. Besides, I need to get out of the house by myself. It's been a long day." Carolyn and Dougie didn't mean to, but they felt cooped up, too. They were at odds with each other and Mommy needed a break from their bickering.

Mommy took her red umbrella with her. She had on a rain jacket that went to her knees, a kerchief on her head, and Daddy's rubber boots on her feet.

Dougie and Carolyn watched for the cows from the double doors at the end of the barn that led out to the barnyard. It was difficult to see very far since the rain was heavy.

They heard the cow bells before they saw them coming. Doug hollered at Daddy when they saw the first one come over the hill of the gravel pit. The cows crossed the brook and started the hard trek through the muddy barnyard. When they stepped in it they sank almost up to their bellies in the mud.

"Have you seen your mother yet?" Daddy asked.

"Here she comes now. I can see her red umbrella," Dougie answered. Carolyn stretched up on her tiptoes, but she still couldn't find Mommy among the cows.

Mommy started to come down the gravel pit. Most of the cows were in front of her, but some were trailing behind. One of the cows didn't like Mommy. Whenever she could she would try to butt Mommy in the stomach. However, Mommy was wise to her wicked ways so she made certain that the cow was in front of her at all times, never behind.

The cow's name was Dolly, a very unsuitable name for such a disreputable animal.

"I hope your Mother realizes that she can't cross that barnyard in its present condition." Daddy was watching with them at the barnyard door with a quizzical smile on his face. The cows were slogging their way through the mud, their legs were covered with it.

Mommy crossed the brook. Daddy went further out on the ramp for a better view. Dougie and Carolyn followed.

"She's not going to turn," he said. "She's not heading for the road, she's coming in the same way the cows are."

Mommy started across the barnyard. Her boot sank deep into the mire. She tried to free herself, but the boot was stuck. She placed the umbrella under her arm and bent over. With the red umbrella sticking out in front she tugged at the boot to loosen it.

Dolly stopped too. She looked back at Mommy. She had been keeping an eye on Mommy all the way home.

Mommy managed to free herself only to take a step forward into the same problem. She looked longingly toward the road, cursing her stupidity in not realizing earlier that she couldn't possibly walk through the barnyard. She was stranded.

Daddy, Dougie and Carolyn had retreated into the barn so the cows could come in out of the rain. Carolyn and Doug fastened the stanchions against the cow's necks while Daddy began the task of washing them down with soapy water.

Meanwhile, Mommy was trying to work her boot loose. "Ray," she yelled. "Ray, where are you? Ray?"

Dolly wasn't going toward the barn any more. She was watching Mommy, who wasn't getting any closer to the barn either.

Suddenly, Mommy's and the cow's eyes met. Mommy knew she was in trouble. She started to yell for help even louder than before.

Against the din of mooing inside the barn and the rain beating on the tin roof no one heard Mommy's desperate cry for help.

Several hectic minutes passed in the barn before Daddy realized that both Dolly and Mommy were still missing.

"I wonder how your mother is making out."

He went out on the ramp to see for himself. Dolly had turned around. She was facing Mommy with her head down. Mommy was using her umbrella like a sword, only the color of the red umbrella had soured Dolly's disposition even further.

Realizing the danger Mommy was in Daddy grabbed his raincoat and galoshes. He ran down the road. When he reached the brook he jumped in, than ran along beside it.

Mommy was using her umbrella to try to scare Dolly away. So far it had worked, but Mommy didn't know how much longer she could keep it up. The cow had grown increasingly hostile.

Daddy picked a couple of small stones out of the brook. He chucked one at Dolly's tough hide, then a second one. "Go on, get out of here," he said, waving his arms at her.

She turned around in the mud and headed for the barn. She hated Mommy, but she loved Daddy. She would do anything he told her to do.

Daddy helped Mommy pull her boots free. He held her elbow while he led her toward the road. By the time they reached the barn he was chuckling.

"Old Dolly sure had you pinned."

"Oh, shut up," Mommy said. "It might be funny to you, but I'm the one she has a grudge against." She was so relieved to be on hard ground again that she was only pretending to be insulted.

When Daddy came in the barn he didn't need to ask the kids if they had seen it. He could tell by the way they were laughing.

"Dolly was the last one to come in," Dougie reported.

"That's because she didn't want to leave your mother," Daddy said, with a twinkle in his eye.

"Go ahead and laugh," Mommy said, but she was laughing, too.

> *Don't be impatient. Wait for the Lord, and He will come and save you! Be brave, stout-hearted, and courageous. Yes, wait and He will help you.* Psalms 27:14a

Chapter 29

Wedding Bells

Uncle Allie and Aunt Dorrie were visiting. The kitchen was noisy, filled with talk and laughter.

Aunt Dorrie's oldest son, Jr., was getting married soon. He and his bride-to-be had sought out a quiet spot in the living room where they could be alone.

Carolyn was curious about weddings. Two of her other cousins were getting married also. They were the twins, Darlene and Dale, Aunt Mabel and Uncle Homer's daughters. They were thirteen years older than their little brother, Duane.

Carolyn knew that one was getting married before the other by four months, but Jr.'s wedding came first.

Carolyn left the noisy kitchen. She wanted to talk to Jr. and June. She didn't understand how a man and a woman could fall in love. When she watched them together they were what Mommy called "moonie-eyed." When she asked what that meant Mommy explained that they only had eyes for each other.

Carolyn had noticed that look in their eyes. It was like their eyes shone. It was curious. None of the married people acted that way. They didn't need to be together every minute, holding hands or kissing.

Falling in love was very confusing.

Carolyn found Jr. and June standing in front of the kerosene stove. Jr. was leaning back against it and June was in his arms. The stove wasn't on because it was a warm day in May.

Carolyn saw them kiss. It looked funny to her because it lasted so long. Whenever Mommy and Daddy kissed it was short and quick.

She walked up to them and stood silently waiting for them to notice her.

"Hi, Carolyn," June said finally. Her face turned a light shade of pink.

Carolyn talked to them for a little while before going back out to the kitchen where there was more activity. When she left they were kissing again.

Later, after the company had left, Mommy took Carolyn aside to talk to her. She wanted to phrase what she had to tell her daughter in such a way as to leave the decision up to Carolyn, but she wanted to present all the facts to her clearly.

"Honey, Jr. and June want you to be the flower girl at their wedding."

"What's that?"

Mommy explained how the flower girl walks down the aisle with a boy who is the ring bearer. It was the custom at large weddings.

Carolyn was very excited. She wanted to wear a fancy dress and hold a bouquet like the bride's, only smaller.

But Mommy hadn't gotten to the bad part yet. "If you decide to be in the wedding it will mean that for the whole week before the wedding you would have to live at Uncle Allie's."

"With you?" Carolyn was remembering what it had been like to stay with Mim and Pip when Doug had his tonsils out.

"No, I have to stay here with Daddy and Doug. You would have to go by yourself."

"Why do I have to be there a whole week?"

"Well, for dress fittings, rehearsals, and all the other details that go into making a wedding day special."

"Can't Daddy take me to those things from here?"

"No, honey. Daddy can't take the time to drive you back and forth that often. If I could drive it would be different. But Daddy has to work. He can't wait with you for hours. No, if you want to be in the wedding you have to stay at Uncle Allie's for the whole week before."

"I want to be in the wedding, Mommy."

"Well, then, you'd better think about it. If you think you can live with them for a week and not get homesick, then you can be in the wedding."

Carolyn did think about it. In fact it was all she thought about. She wanted so much to be in the wedding. It sounded like such fun. June thought she would make a very pretty flower girl, Mommy had told her. She and Jr. wanted her to be in the wedding, but to live with Uncle Allie for a whole week; to be gone from the farm, from Mommy and Daddy. It was a hard choice.

After two days Carolyn made her decision.

"I guess I won't be in the wedding. I don't want to stay with Uncle Allie." She loved Aunt Dorrie, but Uncle Allie, with his loud voice, scared her.

"I think you've made the right decision." Mommy placed a hand on Carolyn's shoulder. She was relieved that Carolyn had made that choice. It would be so much easier this way.

On the day of the wedding Mommy and Daddy hurried to reach the church on time, but it didn't matter because the wedding got started late. It was past eleven before the processional began with the flower girl and ring bearer in the lead.

The flower girl had golden curls. She wore a layered pink dress with a lace bodice. She had Baby's Breath on one side of her hair. She carried a bouquet of pink and white miniature carnations.

Carolyn watched with envious eyes. Now that the actual wedding was taking place Carolyn regretted her decision to not stay with Aunt Dorrie and Uncle Allie. She wished with all her heart to be walking up the aisle with her black hair in ringlets, wearing the pretty pink dress and white shoes, carrying the bouquet of flowers.

"Isn't she darling?" she heard a lady in the seat ahead of her whisper. Would she be saying that if it were me there instead? Carolyn wondered.

The procession of bridesmaids came next. They wore a rainbow of colors. Finally, came the bride. Her father had died the year before so she made the trip down the aisle alone.

June was wearing a long white gown. She had on a veil that billowed out in front of her face each time she took a breath. When she walked past, Carolyn could see that the train that was attached to the waist on the back of the full skirt dragged on the floor behind her. It was a beautiful gown.

The reception that followed was very formal. Carolyn sat at a long table with many people, but she and Doug were seated in the middle of Mommy and

Daddy. There were so many people that she didn't know. Mommy said they were the bride's family.

After the meal was served they cut the wedding cake. For Carolyn it was the only thing on the menu that tasted good.

They cleared the tables to make room for the dancing that followed. The first dance was for the bride and groom. Carolyn watched in rapture. They were so much in love. She hoped that someday a man would look at her that way.

Daddy was starting to rattle the change in his pocket. Mommy reached out her hand to him. She whispered in his ear, he nodded his head.

"It's getting late. Let's go." Carolyn obeyed. When she left Mommy said she could take one of the paper napkins from the table. It had Jr. and June's names on it, the date, and an imprint of a bride and groom. It was her keepsake of this day.

On the weekend of the Fourth of July Carolyn went to her second wedding. Darlene, one of the twins was getting married.

Carolyn watched the processional. It was very much the same as the other wedding, only this time Uncle Homer walked Darlene down the aisle to her intended, Al.

During the high Mass Carolyn could hear Aunt Mabel sniffling from the front row. She kept dabbing at her eyes with a small handkerchief. At the end of the ceremony the priest solemnly declared them man and wife. Al lifted the veil on Dar's wedding gown. As Aunt Mabel blew her nose the bride and groom sealed their promise to each other with a kiss.

This time the wedding was held earlier in the day. At the reception the food was served buffet style.

Carolyn didn't like much of what was served. She was looking forward to the wedding cake. It was too bad that they couldn't serve ice cream with it. Mommy had explained to her that ice cream didn't go with a formal wedding.

The band played the first waltz for the bride and groom. The second waltz was for the bride to dance with her father while the groom danced with his mother. On the third waltz the three couples danced with their partners. After that everyone joined in.

Carolyn squirmed with excitement. She was having a hard time sitting still. She watched Daddy bow to Mommy when he asked her for the next waltz.

They danced three times. Carolyn thought they were the best dancers on the floor.

When Daddy escorted Mommy back to her chair Carolyn jumped to her feet. "Dance with me now, Daddy," she said. She grabbed his hands and began to pull him toward the dance floor. She was aware of Mommy's relatives laughing because they thought she was cute.

She looked way up into Daddy's face. He was smiling at her. She tried to dance, but she was all over the floor. He made her stop.

"Stand on my shoes," he said. He held her right hand, he placed her left hand on his arm. He put his other hand on her waist.

They danced the whole waltz. Daddy was handsome in his blue suit. Carolyn loved him so much she thought her heart would burst.

"Isn't that cute, Ray's dancing with Carolyn."

"Isn't that just like Ray to dance with his daughter."

"Pearl, isn't she cute? Look how she's standing on Ray's feet."

"He's doing all the work."

She didn't care what the relatives were saying. Daddy was dancing with her and she loved him for it.

When they finished the dance he escorted her back to her seat just like he had Mommy.

The third wedding was in the fall.

Mommy was very upset when she read the invitation. This time the children weren't allowed to attend the reception.

"What am I going to do? I have to go to the wedding. I can't attend one of the twin's wedding and not the other one, otherwise there will be hurt feelings. I know Leonard is from a big family and money is tight, but I can't leave Doug and Carolyn home alone for a whole day. I don't have anyone else who I can leave them with, they'll all be at the wedding too."

Daddy had a solution. On the day of the wedding the four of them went to the church. They arrived late so they were seated at the far end of the pew. Carolyn couldn't see much of the processional. She had a quick glimpse of Dale's white gown as she floated past on Uncle Homer's arm.

Aunt Mabel sniffled her way through her second daughter's wedding as the priest droned on.

After the ceremony, instead of going to the reception, Daddy took his family to a restaurant.

Carolyn had never been out to eat before. It was different being in a room full of strangers, each seated at their own small table. Daddy said they could order anything they wanted on the menu.

"Even dessert?"

"Yes, Carolyn, after dinner you can even order dessert."

What fun it was to eat out, although it didn't taste

anywhere near as good as the food Mommy made. Even Daddy said so.

> *An old man's grandchildren are his crowning glory. A child's glory is her father.*
> Proverbs 17:6

Chapter 30

❦

The Deer Hunters

Daddy didn't post his land against hunters.

He didn't have to. Whenever someone wanted to go hunting in his woods they came to the house to ask permission. It was the right thing to do.

When Daddy was younger he use to hunt, but only to provide food for his mother's table. He was a straight shot, but he didn't like to kill animals for sport. However, he didn't mind if other people did.

In November deer season started. Mommy warned Carolyn to stay close to the house. Many inexperienced hunters would be in the woods. Some of them would shoot at anything that moved before they had time to see what it was they were actually shooting at. Accidents like that happened every year.

Carolyn felt sorry for the poor deer. Mommy said that they seemed to have a sixth sense about deer season. All summer and fall the deer were in the meadow or along the edge of the tree line. When deer season came they headed for the high country.

Every day the hunters came. Once in a while the family could hear shots being fired. On weekends they had eight or ten cars or trucks parked along the road in front of the house.

Some who came were relatives. They were the lucky ones. They could hunt in the woods until they were cold or tired. Then they could come down to get warm by Mommy's fire and eat the good food she had prepared.

Then, there was always the hunters who drove slowly by, looking toward the woods hoping for a glimpse of a deer some other hunter had flushed out into the open so they could pull out their rifle and shoot him from the road. Of course, that was illegal, but they did it anyway.

Daddy kept his cows in the barn where he knew they would be safe. He had heard of several cases where an excited hunter shot a farmer's cow in his haste to make a kill.

It was against the law to hunt after dark. Carolyn was happy at the end of each day when the hunters began to come out of the woods without a kill. She knew the deer that she had watched eating grass in the meadow during the summer months were safe for another day.

On the second weekend of deer season it snowed during the night. Saturday morning the hunters came out in droves hoping that the snow would make it easier for them to track down a deer.

Mommy made baked beans for supper. They cooked in her oven for six hours before they were done. The house was filled with the fragrant scent.

Daddy put a ladle full on Carolyn's plate. She covered them with white sugar. It dissolved quickly into the hot beans. Then Daddy poured just a touch of vinegar on them.

Carolyn took a bite. They were so well done they melted in her mouth. She wasn't allowed to use a knife yet so Daddy buttered a slice of bread for her. She dipped it into the brown liquid on her plate from the beans. The corner of the bread absorbed the liquid and turned brown. She raised it to her mouth . . . mmmm. She had been looking forward to this all day.

The temperature outside was dropping. It had been a cold day, but it was going to be an even colder night. It was very dark out, but the kitchen was warm and bright with the good smell of beans.

They were surprised when there was a knock on the door. A young man, shivering in the wool red and black plaid suit that hunters wore in the woods, stood on the threshold. When he took his hat off his brown hair was matted against his head. He had an open, honest face, but his brown eyes were troubled. His mouth was turned down. He looked exhausted to the point of falling down.

"Good evening, sir. I'm sorry to interrupt your meal, but could you tell us where we are? My friend and me got turned around in the woods and now we can't find our way back to the car."

"Come in." Daddy opened the door wider to the stranger.

"No, thank you just the same. I don't want to get your floor wet. You see, when we realized we were lost we started to follow the brook hoping it would lead us to a road. After dark, when we couldn't see the brook clearly, we got in so we wouldn't lose it. I'm awful wet."

"All the more reason for you to come in out of the cold. Is that your friend by the road? Call to him so the two of you can get warm by the fire."

"I don't think that's such a good idea, sir." The young man lowered his voice. "You see, my friend got real scared out in the woods when we knew we were lost. Well, the fact of the matter is, he's been crying. He's ashamed to be seen in the light. If you could just give me directions we'll be on our way."

"Where did you start from?" Daddy asked.

The young man told him.

"My God, that road is in Richmond. Do you mean to say you took the woods from there and you've been in them ever since? You must be dead on your feet."

"We've been walking since 5:00 this morning, sir."

"If you'd followed the road instead of zig-zagging through the forest you would have gotten here by breakfast. We're only three miles from town." Daddy was incredulous.

He added, "I'll drive you back to your car." Daddy started to get his hat and coat, but the young man stopped him with his next words.

"Fact is, we came with two other friends. They went in a different direction. One of them owns the car. He has the keys in his pocket. I don't even know if it will still be where we left it. We were suppose to meet them at noon in the woods for lunch, but we couldn't find the spot where they told us to wait. After we ate we were all going to walk back to the car. I suppose that's what the other two did."

"Have you had anything to eat?" Mommy asked.

"No, ma'am, not since supper last night. I was up too early to be hungry at breakfast and then the other two fellows took the lunch sack with them."

"I'm going to fill a couple of plates up with beans. You and your friend can either come in to eat or, if you'd rather, you can eat outside." Mommy went into the pantry for the plates.

"Why did you pick these woods if you don't know your way around them?" Daddy asked.

"Well, my friend with the car knows them. That's why we came here, but after the first hour we decided we'd separate so we could cover more ground. Only thing is the woods all look the same. We couldn't tell if we were headed north, west or where."

Mommy gave the young man two plates full of the steaming beans along with a couple of slices of buttered bread each. He thanked her and went across the lawn to rejoin his friend.

Daddy and Mommy discussed the situation. "I don't know what to do. If I drive them to town and the car is gone where do I go from there?"

Mommy made a suggestion. "I could ask them to spend the night. Or they can come in to use the telephone to try to locate their friend."

Daddy thought about it before he answered. "What if their friend isn't home yet. Maybe he's still in the woods trying to track them. No, the best thing to do is to bring them both home, back to Burlington or wherever they live. Then they'll be safe, they won't be wandering around in the dark."

The man returned the empty plates. Mommy asked him if they wanted more. "Just a drink of water, if you have it, please."

"Where you from?" Daddy asked while Mommy went to get the water.

"Massachusetts. But we're attending the University of Vermont."

He took the glasses of water Mommy handed him. Wearily he went down the steps. The young man who had waited by the road met him part way. Thirstily they drank the refreshing water.

Suddenly there was a shout from the road. A car had started to drive slowly by when its headlights caught the men. The car stopped. The driver rolled down his window. He began to shout and honk the car horn.

Carolyn and Dougie went to the kitchen window. They could see the men in the light from the car. They could hear the voices, but couldn't discern what was being said.

When the young man returned the water glasses he said, "That's my friend in the car out there." His face was lit up. His eyes were bright. He didn't look scared or discouraged any more.

"How'd he find you?"

"When we didn't show up at the meeting place at dinnertime he figured we were lost. He's been driving around on every back road since."

He thanked Mommy and Daddy for their kindness and ran joyfully across the snow packed yard to join his friends in the waiting car.

Daddy rubbed the back of his head with his hand. "Those two were lucky. Not every inexperienced hunter gets off this easily."

"What do you mean, Daddy?" Douglas asked.

Daddy began to list the problems they could have

run into. "They might have wandered around in those woods for days before finding a way out. They could have fallen off a ledge in the dark. One of them could have broken a leg. Then what would they have done? Without knowing which way to go his friend wouldn't even be able to bring help back to him. They didn't have any food with them.

"They happened across the brook by accident. One of them was smart enough to know that if they followed it downstream it would eventually lead them out of the woods. But it must have been ice cold to walk in. They could get rheumatism or pneumonia from it.

"They were also very lucky to be standing next to the road when that car came over the hill. If they had agreed to eat in here their friend would have driven right past, never realizing how close they were. A few more minutes one way or the other and they would have missed each other altogether."

"They were lucky alright," Mommy agreed. She began to clear the table.

> *Let your eyes look directly forward, and your gaze be straight before you. Take heed to the path of your feet, then all your ways will be sure. Do not swerve to the right or to the left; turn your foot away from evil.*
> Proverbs 4:25-27